Collateral DAMAGE

Collateral
DAMAGE

The Imperiled Status of Truth in American Public Discourse and Why It Matters to You

JAY R. HARMAN

authorHOUSE®

AuthorHouse™
1663 Liberty Drive
Bloomington, IN 47403
www.authorhouse.com
Phone: 1-800-839-8640

Published by AuthorHouse 1/31/2014

ISBN: 978-1-4918-5572-0 (sc)
ISBN: 978-1-4918-5573-7 (e)

Library of Congress Control Number: 2014901129

For Theresa, Sara, and Rachel,
to leave them the better parts of myself.

Contents

Introduction and Overview

The 2008 presidential election campaign between candidates Barack Obama and John McCain was a particularly bruising battle that may have set new low-water marks for negativity. Not only was the contest replete with personal rather than issue-centered ads, the McCain campaign (which one observer for *Time* characterized as "uniquely dishonest") so often distorted or misrepresented certain campaign issues that the goal seemed to be little more than winning the election at all costs. And those costs were high indeed, not only in terms of dollars spent but also with regard to the basic credibility of the campaign messages. Fundamentally, it was open season on the ethic of honesty itself, and, unfortunately, the 2012 presidential campaign delivered only more of the same.

Such behavior appeared to reach its full development in the venomous public debate leading up to the passage of the health care reform bill in March 2010. Opponents of the bill characterized it in the most dire terms, claiming that it would take away choice in the health marketplace, lead to death panels that would pull the plug on grandma, and start the Europeanization of America (presumably, a reference to creeping socialism). All of these claims were flat-out exaggerations or worse. Moreover, these same opponents pointed to polls purporting to show that a majority of Americans opposed the bill, which they said justified their own opposition to it. Ironically, missing from this debate was any honest acknowledgment that their own very vocal and coordinated distortions of the bill's provisions might have contributed to the public's negative view of it in the first place.

Unfortunately, the disinformation that infected this particular public policy discussion was only one example of what seems to be a growing practice in the public arena. Perhaps one of the most telling examples during the early part of the Obama administration was the confusion that swirled around the subject of the president's religion, with allegations mostly from conservatives that he was a Muslim. While polls indicated that broad sectors of the public harbored some uncertainty about this matter, more than twice as many of those self-identifying as Republicans held this view despite its denial by fact-checking sources on the Internet and virtually no corroboration from mainstream news media. How could such an incorrect belief have arisen or been perpetuated? Most who held this view reportedly claimed that they heard it in "the media," but only right-wing outlets were voicing it.

In his widely acclaimed book *The Republican War on Science*, Chris Mooney examined the antiscience, anti-intellectual bias of the George W. Bush administration and found that it contaminated both their practices and policies to the detriment of broader American interests at home and abroad. While I would like to say that, unlike the Republican war on science, the tendency toward negativity and dishonest public discourse is a curse on both major political parties, after the recent campaign I think that the Republicans, under the initial guidance of prominent tacticians such as Lee Atwater and more recently Karl Rove, seem to have perfected the genre.

Regrettably, with the intense interest in the outcome of the 2010 midterm election and the perception that so much was at stake, such practices continued full-throttle in the fall campaign and to an even larger extent in the 2012 presidential election. These practices prompt us to ask about their ill effects. After so much distortion of facts and circulation of outright lies during the campaign, what are the lingering consequences? Do those who orchestrate these practices really think that, after the votes are cast, everybody suffers amnesia? What about possible deeper corrosion to the overall ethic of respect for truthfulness or even the *morality* of such practices?

While we all may find the practices distasteful, I view them as more than a personal annoyance, with considerably higher stakes. This is because such tactics as spin, exaggeration, misrepresentation, and flat-out untruthfulness may come with significant political and social costs that at the very least compromise the integrity of the voting process on which a healthy democracy depends.

These are not trivial and emerge if the resulting public misinformation and obfuscation distort our collective judgment about which version of objective truth is best supported. Decisions we need to make as public citizens, for example, may then be compromised because we are thinking incorrectly about impacts of policy on various sectors of the population, particularly minorities and the disadvantaged, or we are inaccurately assessing public risk from such threats as global climate change. How can effective public policy be formulated if the electorate itself is so confused that it cannot express an informed opinion at the polls? If, for example, a large minority of conservative voters is misinformed about something as straightforward as a president's religion, how can they be expected to express a thoughtful judgment on more complex matters such as tax or health-care proposals, or global climate change (which they do by choosing among different candidates at the polls)?

In addition, social costs emerge if such practices undermine respect for the principle of honesty that the wider society may esteem and require for smooth functioning. At the same time, misleading the public for purposes of short-term political gain raises unsettling ethical questions, particularly for a political party that wraps itself in the embrace of "family values" and sees no hypocrisy in the practice. All in all, I think it should be clear from these considerations that the various forms of untruthfulness that so often comprise political discourse in America today (and no more so than in debates about global warming and health care) at least *have the potential* for wide and underappreciated adverse effects across our society.

I quickly concede that, at first glance, we all might be forgiven for whatever casual transgressions of honesty we sometimes commit, because in some respects truth-telling is one of the most challenging of our moral norms to comply with. Nonetheless, it is a prominent virtue essential to human society, and for compelling reasons. Most importantly, it is at the heart of communication between us: generally, we each strive to say what we mean, mean what we say, and assume others do likewise. This assumption amounts to an unspoken contractual understanding that is nothing less than the basis for that communication. Without it, we would end up either expending unnecessary energy verifying the truthfulness of everyone else's communication (verbal or otherwise) or be uncertain about just whom or what to believe. Either way, our ability to converse would be seriously undermined.

In fact, many observers, even including the esteemed philosopher Immanuel Kant, have long recognized that social intercourse would become next to impossible without an assumption of truthfulness (Frankfurt 2006). Kant went so far as to claim that falsehoods not only offend others and besmirch the reputation of the untruthful, they also "threaten the order of society" (Frankfurt 2006, 74). As a result, truthfulness seems to be a character dimension esteemed in all societies, one that we trust each other to respect and cultivate, and for good reasons.

Despite these reasons, however, in some types of communicative endeavors we still seem quite willing to stretch, selectively omit, distort, or otherwise take liberties with the prevailing conceptions of truth. Doing so in our personal relationships might harm others we care about (not to mention our own reputation), but we seem less hesitant to do it when the victims are anonymous or unknown to us. As noted above, folk wisdom has it that such practices virtually define politics, particularly as it has been on display recently.

Why we do it is not always clear, although in a political context the shape of the calculation appears plain enough: if we are being rational and reflective, we judge that the expected gains exceed the costs. In this book, however, one of my central claims is that assessing such costs is problematic because they are often obscure and multifaceted, which leads to their underestimation. For example, as a politician I may be fully cognizant of the extent to which such acts reflect back on me personally and be perfectly willing to take the risk associated with being untruthful, while being completely unaware of their other *unintended* consequences, such as the complex and indirect manner in which they may harm others. As a candidate for elected office, I might very well conclude that making false promises or embellishing my record is worth whatever harm is spread across an anonymous, faceless electorate if it wins me an election. The point here is that without personal knowledge of the full harms my misleading and untruthful public claims have created, I could easily downplay this harm in my calculation.

Furthermore, we often choose to ignore social pressures that normally hold such behavior in check, or they are offset by other incentives. We seem more willing to overlook lapses of veracity when we otherwise esteem and perhaps want to emulate the guilty party. In addition, when untruthfulness is encountered frequently, we may become inured to it or even come to expect it, and it loses its traditional stigma. Carried to its logical end, such evolving acceptance could then become a new social norm.

Unfortunately, such a development can have serious social implications. The greatest of these may be *the erosion of trust*. If we come to the point of disbelieving what others tell us, then we may also begin to question the authenticity of their overall behavior, and the causal link between untruthfulness and undermined trust is established. Trust, meanwhile, is a lynchpin of a free civil society. It adds reciprocal predictability to our behavior and reassures each of us that others will adhere on their own to customs and norms that we value, with minimal coercion or oversight. Without it, behavior will have to be regulated (if we desire some degree of social order) by extrinsic measures such as laws (accompanied by police surveillance) and economic incentives that restrict personal freedom and/or create various other costs, which can be sizable. Although the particular transaction costs we all bear to redress these impacts are not my sole concern here, they often seem neglected in discussions of why public morality matters and represent a potential form of collateral damage missing from discussions of the costs of untruthfulness in the public sphere.

In addition, by reinforcing the ethic of truth-telling, as well as by increasing the probability that claims circulated among us are well-supported, a public ethic that respects truth and truthfulness helps us as individuals to avoid the many costs associated with acting on false beliefs if, for example, they lead us to pursue strategies that are inconsistent with our objectives. At the same time, holding false beliefs raises serious ethical issues when they form the basis for choices that end up harming others or allow us as an electorate to support political views with ultimately adverse consequences (such as the World War II internment of Japanese Americans or the pursuit of our military campaign in Iraq). In sum, I think that the potential for far-reaching negative impacts (both political and social) associated with a public ethic that vitiates truthfulness is not only sizable but also largely unrecognized in America today.

Opening up a conversation about this matter, of course, requires that I first stake out some basic philosophical positions. The primary one concerns the existence and nature of truth, even the mention of which probably sends some readers who suspect a troubling turn to discarded Enlightenment philosophy and antirelativist argument scrambling for the exits. Nonetheless, the need for full (and advance) disclosure requires that I indicate that, while this piece is not intended to be a discourse in philosophy, it does indeed rest on a philosophical conviction that objective truth exists and that more or less truthful accounts can be distinguished by greater or lesser amounts of evidence. We are talking about "empirical" truths here.

In order to work our way through this conversation, I have broken it down into five principal sections. The first, "Some Preliminary Remarks," is the briefest of them all and lays out some basic definitions of such words as "truth" and "truthfulness" as they will be used here. I harbor no delusions about plowing fresh philosophical earth in this section but merely seek to clarify the terms of our discussion so that the conversation can take place. In the following section, "The Costs of Untruthfulness," I attempt to justify this effort by arguing that many of these specific costs are both hidden and sizable. Consequences such as eroded trust, undermined democracy, the engendering of false beliefs, economic costs, and associated ripple effects are each considered in their own subsections. The next section, "Why Truthfulness Challenges Us," is an exploration of both why we find untruthfulness so easy to commit and what incentives we encounter that invite us to engage in it. Several specific ones are considered, such as the "imperative of the present," which is our apparently deep-seated tendency to respond to immediate, local challenges before more distant, diffuse ones. While I view this "imperative" as a factor that complicates our adherence to *all* moral principles, I look at other incentives, also, that are specific to untruthfulness. This section examines the oft-raised possibility that engaging in market transactions, now so much a part of modern commerce, inevitably undermines our willingness to be truthful by virtue of the degree to which the "principle of minimal sufficiency" permeates those transactions. I also examine the possible impact of marketing and advertising practices on our truthfulness ethic, the emergence of special interest groups that disseminate slanted or biased information disguised as objective content, the tendency for perks and profits to accompany elected office, and the impact of the Internet as a source of news and views as both a positive and negative influence, each in their own subsections.

The fourth major section of this piece, "The Many Forms of Untruthfulness," uses sometimes contemporary events or controversies to illustrate several common forms that untruthful discourse assumes. Such practices as the use of "spin," the declaration of unsupported claims as true and/or the rejection of any evidence contrary to our claims out of fear of its implications, epistemological absolutism (clinging to one view of things come what may), hypocrisy, and several forms of fallacious reasoning all get their turn. The fifth section, "Addressing the Problem," is an attempt to take this critique into positive territory by laying out some possible remedies. I begin by distinguishing between intrinsic and extrinsic motivation to prompt adherence to moral principles and argue that relying on the former offers us several advantages compared to relying on the latter. That said, I consider the importance of maintaining public vigilance concerning public untruthfulness, increasing the resources available to research universities as a way to discourage the use of tainted, agenda-driven research funding, maintaining a free and independent press, including critical thinking in our school curricula, and nurturing a broader self-interest conception across our society.

The last major section of this piece continues focusing on the theme of possible remedies by examining the usefulness of religious instruction to promote greater adherence to such moral virtues as truthfulness. It is included here because religious instruction is *not* one of the avenues I suggest in the previous section (and one we might expect to find included in such a list of possible remedies). In this section, I view at least certain forms of religion as providing just one more form of extrinsic motivation, which we earlier concluded was a more costly, less effective route to moral compliance than was intrinsic motivation. The many epistemological/logical difficulties inherent in religious claims and the problems that I argue are created in other areas of our decision making by our embracing such claims are also surveyed. Finally, I conclude this section by reflecting on whether the suspension of analytical processes sometimes associated with the embrace of religious beliefs, particularly the most literal ones, is related to our aggregate willingness (or unwillingness) as a society to accept standard scientific theories (such as evolution) and embrace scientific literacy as a desirable social goal.

Listening to discussions of "family values" and morality among many of our public figures today, we might sometimes conclude that the only morals we should be concerned about are applied in the bedroom, brothel, or abortion clinic. I believe such an analysis is a gross oversimplification that fails to take into account what I contend are the far larger harms from other forms of questionable behavior, especially playing fast and loose with the truth in the public arena.

As should be obvious, I engage in this discussion convinced that rational discourse and discussion can by itself change people's behavior by changing their minds. When people know better, they will do better, we are told. Part of "knowing better" in the first place is simply coming to understand that we are causing harm. I have no doubt that a decline in the overall level of respect accorded the ethic of truthfulness would, in time, leave most of us worse off, and I hope that opening such a conversation about the matter is a constructive step in halting and perhaps reversing that decline.

Because the range of topics taken up in this discussion is considerable, my aim in this manuscript is only to introduce the main themes and arguments and to show how they might fit together in a coherent view of the problem. Many of the individual sections are sketchy and include only the broad and essential points, and I leave to others the task of fleshing out the details or supporting evidence. At the same time, I have included only a few citations to relevant supporting material in order to concentrate on the flow of the central argument(s).

Plant taxonomists joke that some of their kind are "lumpers," preferring to combine taxonomic groupings where possible in their quest for elegance and simplicity, whereas others are "splitters" who relish the detail and precision of their science. As a geographer, I fall more in the first category, and in this piece I trust that I have included at least enough detail to allow the shape of the thesis I am advancing to emerge, while avoiding unnecessary digressions into distracting minutia.

1 Some Preliminary Remarks

In a discussion of this type, an early decision any author faces is exactly where to pick up the narrative, or where, basically, the story or argument begins. In this case, I want to open with a few introductory remarks about language and the notion of truth.

An essential facet of what make us all human is our capacity to think symbolically, which then helps make possible our marvelous communicative skills. While we each use these skills in pursuit of many different communicative objectives, in order for verbal communication of any kind to occur we must have mutually recognized definitions and syntactical relationships between terms. Such definitions and relationships are based on a wider consensus within our community about facets of our language, which is necessary in order for our communicative acts to be interpretable by others. Establishing the necessary community-based meanings and syntaxes, in turn, requires some method of verification so that disputes about them can be resolved. Normally, such verification

1

has an empirical component that permits the meanings of our terms to be tethered to sensory experiences. For example, if you and I disagree about what an utterance that sounds like "table" means, one of us can point to such an object and establish the connection. Eventually, others would come to agree with this definition of the utterance of "table," and it becomes the accepted version. Through such a process, the notion of *truth*, that symbolic version of the objective world favored by most members of our community, ultimately emerges.

As straightforward as such an account may seem, just what counts as "truth" is in fact a contentious philosophical question today (at least among some quarters), and as a result one does not wade into a discussion of the term without some trepidation. In order to avoid getting entangled in it, I will ask your forbearance and sidestep much of this debate so that we can cut to the heart of the important issues. In so doing, I assume that we can agree, along with Frankfurt (2006, 11), on a commonsense understanding of terms such as "truth" and "falsity." The justification for this step is that, while we may not be able to exactly define these terms, we nonetheless share a common understanding of the difference between them and routinely trade in a vocabulary that requires us to draw distinctions of certitude and truthfulness, particularly when we work in fields such as science and law. As a result, I include here only some very rough comments on the matter to show where I stand on the debate so that the overall discussion in this piece can move forward.

Obviously, "untruthfulness" and "truthfulness" are different sides of the same behavioral coin, and the recognition of one requires that we be able to distinguish it from examples of the other. Fundamentally, it is a feature of transactions between cognitively competent humans in which an understanding of the objective world is assumed or conveyed. In this discussion, untruthfulness is used to denote *deceitful communicative behavior* or, more simply, communicative misrepresentation. This definition is intended to distinguish such communication from that which is merely erroneous (that is, it *accidentally* conveys a nonstandard truth conception).

Because our definition of "untruthfulness" concerns acts that are intended to convey partial or distorted (and certainly nonstandard) conceptions of things, in theory it could be expanded to include acts that are not primarily communicative in nature, such as the failure to keep expressed or implied commitments or even to be authentic with oneself. Indeed, most of us would likely hold these kinds of actions to be another form of untruthfulness anyway. Out of fear about getting off track, however, I want to focus on what are intended to be communicative acts rather than widening the circle to include other forms of behavior.

Most commonly, the motive behind untruthfulness appears to be personal gain or the avoidance of loss. As a result, it assumes many forms. Some forms can be deflective (to avoid blame-laying for wrongdoing, such as Bill Clinton's now infamous line, "I did not have sex with that woman ...") or embellishment (when achievements or actions are portrayed in better light than they warrant); frequently, it consists of "half-truths" when some details are willfully omitted to slant the meaning being conveyed, or of flat-out hyperbole or exaggeration spun, ultimately, to influence the behavior of others. Recently, for example, we have seen several documented instances when members of Congress distorted the nature of their military service in the presence of audiences that were likely to be impressed by such service.

"Being truthful" has both ethical and epistemological components. The ethical dimension arises because the "truthful" person intends to tell the truth; one would intend to mean what one conveys and intend that what is conveyed corresponds to a generally accepted objective state of affairs in some way. Epistemological considerations arise, as well, because the agent needs to have an *accurate enough understanding* of things in the objective world in order to produce an acceptable and intelligible rendering of it, an assumption that raises questions about methods of inquiry. In addition, she needs to be sufficiently intellectually competent to be able to communicate what is meant. If all these conditions obtain, then others can agree that she is characterizing it accurately and apparently intends to do so. In short, she is being truthful.

Such a commonsense analysis of these distinctions offers some interesting insights. We would likely regard someone who both aspires to be factually accurate and actually succeeds at doing so as "truthful," but absent factual accuracy and in the presence of good intention she would likely just be considered to be "mistaken." The act of making factually correct utterances without the *intention* to do so, however, seems to have no specific lingual denotation, probably because a *pattern* of accidental accuracy is an unlikely outcome in the first place. Meanwhile, factual inaccuracy coupled with the intention to be factually inaccurate would in most settings likely earn a pejorative characterization (perhaps as "deception"). Given the harsher characterization of intentional versus unintentional error, the implication seems to be that we are more willing to overlook failures of analysis than deficiencies of intent (associated with the willful purveying of factual inaccuracies, in this case). That is, we seem to be saying that only purveying bad information intentionally has an unethical dimension to it.

2 The Costs of Untruthfulness

Why should we care whether we are truthful with each other? Other than being an irritant or annoyance to us, precisely why should untruthfulness of a neighbor or, more specifically, a particular elected official or advocacy group be a concern? I think there are at least four reasons, and all derive their importance from more basic values. Fundamentally, untruthfulness does harm because (1) it may undermine a sense of trust among members in society that is necessary for the operation or observance of other social functions, (2) it distracts us from forming and holding true beliefs, (3) it risks undermining our mutual commitment to other moral values in something of a "ripple effect," and (4) adopting measures to offset it diverts resources from other pursuits, creating important externalities and opportunity costs. Obviously, then, the degree of concern we might have about this overall problem depends directly on how serious we think the consequences of untruthfulness are, that is, how much we esteem a trusting and trustworthy society, what the merits of holding and acting on true belief are, how we value other unintended effects of untruthfulness, and what we see as the costs of repairing its damage. In other words, the importance of truthfulness piggybacks onto these other social goods at least to the extent that its absence necessitates remedial costs, and one may argue that its importance is derived from and proportional to them. In a strong sense, these costs represent a form of collateral damage from untruthfulness rarely discussed or even acknowledged. Let's consider them each in turn.

Eroded Trust

Being truthful concerns a triangular relationship between ourselves, truth, and those around us. Briefly, if I acquire a reputation for being "truthful," others will trust me to fulfill certain behavioral expectations each time they interact with me. When broken down into its requisite components, this expectation amounts to an important and sizable set of functions. First, at a minimum, others will assume that I will continue to define words and use syntactical relationships according to accepted standards so that our communication may continue. Second, they will expect that the content of statements I utter could pass some truthfulness test; that is, they can depend on what I say as achieving some level of empirical reliability, or at least to logically cohere with other such statements that have met such a test. Third, and perhaps most importantly, they will assume good intent, knowing that the two previous conditions could not be routinely met without it. Thus, from truthfulness comes trustworthiness and, ultimately, trust. While no one would be justified in assuming that I always speak the truth (one can always be confused or have bad information, as noted earlier), based on my reputation they could trust that I would attempt to do so. In fact, social science research has shown that truth-telling is generally an assumed feature of our communication that we trust others to observe unless and until we have reasons to suspect otherwise.

We interact with those around us in different ways. Sometimes we physically encounter them or effect change in their lives by what we do at a particular place and time. Mostly, however, we communicate with them by exchanging messages about our feelings, expectations, perceptions, wants, and needs, and by listening to them about theirs. As a result, the realm of communication provides us abundant opportunities to cultivate (or undermine) a sense of trust with them—more so, perhaps, than in any other area of interpersonal interaction. Consequently, I think it is not an overstatement to observe that the communicative realm is virtually a crucible where society's overall sense of interpersonal trust is cultivated and nurtured, as Habermas (1990) seems to be arguing. That is, there is no more basic set of interactions between us than those directed toward communication, and because these attempts at interpersonal communication cannot go on without a sense of trust underpinning them, how we engage in this communication every day may be importantly related to the overall level of trust prevailing within our wider societal setting.

Unfortunately, a variety of national surveys suggest that trust is declining in America. The General Social Survey, which surveys Americans' values and moods, shows a ten-point decline between 1976 and 2000 in the number of Americans who believe other people can generally be trusted. Meanwhile, our trust in institutions is similarly declining; since the 1970s, it has declined from 24 percent to 11 percent in the press and from 26 percent to 17 percent in corporations, and it has even declined in organized religion (from 35 percent to 25 percent). Research conducted in 2001 at Harvard University by the GoodWork Project revealed an "overwhelming distrust of politicians and the political process" by teenagers. While all the causes of this trend are not entirely clear, the degree to which untruthfulness infects political discourse, especially at election time, cannot help matters.

The Benefits of Trust

Meanwhile, trust is the "glue" that holds a society together, and support for that view comes from many quarters, even anecdotal sources. For example, John Barry, author of *The Great Influenza*, in a recent interview on National Public Radio (broadcast on 5 May, 2009, as a part of "Morning Edition") observed that government attempts to play down the severity of the developing influenza outbreak in 1918, out of fears that it would distract from the then-ongoing war effort, left the citizenry feeling betrayed and sowed widespread mistrust, originally of the government, but eventually directed toward many phases of public life. At the level of the individual, furthermore, as we have seen, being able to assume that each of us will be truthful makes communication possible. Habermas, for example, in his elaboration on what he refers to as "discourse ethics," repeatedly emphasizes how "communicative practice of everyday life rests on ... shared propositional knowledge, on normative accord, and on mutual trust" (1990, 136) and on "reciprocity and mutual recognition" (130). At the same time, of course, I can also assume that you will keep your word. As a result, trust underlies virtually all ethical systems because it allows me to assume that (1) others will comply with the relevant principles, and (2) they will do so without coercion even when it sometimes conflicts with their self-interest (forced compliance with a moral code is not what is usually meant by "moral" behavior). Absent such an assumption, our default strategy becomes something akin to Ronald Reagan's (oxymoronic) observation regarding the former Soviet Union's compliance with terms of its nuclear treaties—that is, we need to "trust, but verify." Of course, genuine trust dispenses with the need to verify in the first place.

Undermined Democracy

Obviously, the effectiveness of a democratic government depends on the election (and subsequent performance) of effective legislators, which in turn depends on our making wise choices in the voting booth. In order for us to do so, however, and assuming we cast our ballots for candidates based on an informed judgment about their likely performance once in office, electors must have access to accurate, complete information about both the issues as well as the stances of the various candidates with regard to these issues.

Obfuscation of the issues by equivocation or deception reduces the likelihood of both. Partisan, biased, or blatantly untruthful information challenges even the most informed fraction of the electorate, making it difficult even for them to cast informed votes, while negative campaigning (detached from the issues or based on irrelevant personal qualities of the candidates) appeals to the "gut feelings" of many in the electorate, making a decision based on careful objective analysis of the issues all the more difficult. We each have only so much surplus time and energy to devote to analysis of election issues before we feel overwhelmed by good information, let alone misinformation or campaign distortions. The fear, of course, is that absent good information and an informed electorate, election outcomes would then turn more on personal appeal or emotion than on a rational analysis of the issues or candidates themselves, or voters would disengage from the process altogether by staying home. Sometimes, in a campaign atmosphere already poisoned by negative messages and personal attacks and particularly when the issues are complex and require political initiatives that have both winners and losers, the candidates might be less than forthright about the negative consequences of an initiative. Legitimate occasions for revenue enhancement, for example, might be avoided out of a fear of reprisal by opponents complaining about "tax and spend liberals." As a result, the voters may be deprived of full disclosure or, worse, risk having legitimate political solutions to pressing problems taken off the table prematurely.

The push for health-care reform initiated by the Obama administration in 2009–10 illustrates the problem. What seemed to start as a well-intentioned attempt to address numerous problems in the American health-care delivery system (rising costs, a growing uninsured sector of the population) generated not only legitimate opposition from various stakeholders who saw themselves adversely impacted by the proposed changes but also deceptive and negative response from many Republicans who were bent on defeating such an initiative regardless of its form. While the bill scraped through in the House, where it garnered limited Republican support, its difficulty in the Senate, where not one Republican voted for it, was greater. Meanwhile, opponents were characterizing it in harshest of terms in the media, claiming that it would grow the national debt (an outlook at variance with CBO estimates), result in a government takeover of health care, take away choice in the market place, and increase our taxes. None of these outcomes were based on informed projections, but they certainly resonated with the fears of an uninformed public, one that was relying on what it heard and read in the media for its information. In the midst of the debate, after the Senate passed the bill and as it was about to be reconciled with the version passed earlier from the House, a special election in Massachusetts saw Republican Scott Brown win what had been Edward Kennedy's senate seat. This vote was construed by opponents to reflect deep public dislike for the broad shape of the overall bill; then House minority leader John Boehner referred to it as a bill that "working families just cannot afford and want nothing to do with." Although analyses projected otherwise, and polls suggested that when they understood what the bill would do for them most people were in support of it, the constant drumbeat of fearful rhetoric and misinformation from opponents swamped legitimate public discussion of the bill's many provisions and ultimately prevented, I believe, the public from grasping a thorough understanding of its benefits.

Later polls then revealed further slippage of public support in something of a feedback loop, and in the aftermath some congressional members who had been behind the bill grew increasingly squeamish about it. Ultimately, its future in the courts was for the time being at least assured, but repeal sentiment continued to resonate among Republicans in Congress. Rather than joining the discussion and seeking compromise, the Republicans' use of exaggeration, misinformation, and outright distortion not only hobbled the democratic process by preempting the flow of valuable information to the electorate, crippling their ability to make an informed choice, but doubtlessly also sowing more cynicism toward politicians in general because, in light of the misinformation campaign, supporters of the bill were seen as trying to, well, sell a flawed bill of goods to the American people. Not only were democratic institutions impugned, but the ethic of truthfulness was assailed, as well.

If the sum effect of campaign distortions, smears, and untruths is a flow of information so compromised that it impairs our ability to make reasoned judgments in the polling booth, we are unable to effectively participate in the voting "market" as consumers, and an imperfect market results. The puzzle is why as a society we tolerate market deception in one sector (the political realm) but are less tolerant of it in the economic realm. Defenders of market solutions might argue that the rise of fact-checking groups is a form of market response to this state of affairs that redresses these abuses, much as Consumers Union is a response to a welter of questionable advertising claims. We incur costs from deceptive practices, however, when they force us to seek out and evaluate alternative sources of information. Furthermore, with the development of an increasingly compartmentalized information market in the media and on the Internet, characterized by many different but partisan sources of news and editorials, we can now find versions of the news that agree with, rather than challenge, whatever preexisting biases (no matter how extreme) we might have and, therefore, are more likely to come away with our own prejudices reinforced. Gone are the days when we might be exposed to contrary viewpoints that broaden our perspectives because no other news sources were available.

Meanwhile, trust is a key ingredient to the smooth functioning of a democracy, and if flagrant untruthfulness undermines trust in the political sphere, other unintended consequences may follow. For example, we trust our fellow citizens to be as informed as possible about election issues and to cast informed votes for candidates, which requires that they stay abreast of news and events so that they can be discerning electors. If most elected officials are perceived as dishonest or untrustworthy, however, we may be less motivated to vote for any of them. Unfortunately, as members of a working democracy we trust our neighbors to cast their votes. Otherwise, elections may not reflect the will of the majority. If only motivated extremists vote, for example, we are more likely to end up with extremist governments and government policies that reflect an active minority rather than the far larger "moderate middle," a situation reminiscent of the G. W. Bush years in the White House, when the national vote disproportionately reflected the preferences of an energized conservative evangelical minority.

We also trust our elected officials to keep their oaths of office and to act as our representatives rather than pursue only their narrow self-interests (with an eye on their reelection) at decision time. While some may argue that legislators acting only in their self-interests (by casting votes consistent with the wishes of their constituency to assure their reelection, for example) is exactly how a representative government *ought* to work, such an argument fails to recognize those times when unpopular public policy initiatives are appropriate. A legislator who is always guided by the will of his constituency (and casts votes on the expectation that they will put him in good standing with the majority of voters) is unlikely to lead the electorate into new territory or to display what has come to be regarded as political "vision" if his positions are reactionary. Healthy democracy requires that our leaders at least occasionally lead, rather than follow, and we *trust* them to do so when the public interests are at stake.

Engendering False Beliefs

Why do we occasionally behave in ways that violate what we understand to be moral principles? This nagging, age-old question has many possible answers. Aside from the truly pathological criminal, who lacks the emotional or cognitive mechanisms to fully grasp the consequences of her actions, most of our moral lapses stem from a few major causes.

First, we may lack full knowledge of the consequences of our behavior. We cannot hold a subject responsible for his actions if he is unaware of their consequences (although we may expect that a reasonable effort is made to determine what they might have been). Second, we may not know that our actions violate a widely held ethical principle (perhaps embodied in a legal document), although, again, we may expect that a reasonable effort will have been made to understand the relevant ethical/legal principles. Third, we may lack the affective inclination (the "goodwill" or "character" spoken of by philosophers) to do the right action. Or, alternatively, our actions may be guided by factually erroneous beliefs about those with whom we are interacting, the variables we need to take into account, or the consequences of our actions.

Of the four, this latter problem may be directly related to the quality of information we have at our disposal (i.e., whether it is true or not). Of course, we may choose to believe what we know is untrue or believe falsely even though we think our beliefs are true, but the proposition that we *routinely* choose to do so seems untenable. Alternatively, our decision-making habits may at times be defective or not strenuously enough applied, and we stumble when distinguishing true from false claims. Even more likely, and relevant to our discussion here, our attempts to determine what to believe are challenged by an array of misinformation before us, and we lack the resources or inclination to sort it all out.

Meanwhile, false beliefs, when acted on, cause us as individuals to incur unnecessary costs. If I believe I am well when I am not, my life could be in jeopardy without evasive or mitigative action, and if I believe I am ill when I am well, I am more likely to divert my resources into the care of my health that I could more usefully invest elsewhere. A set of beliefs that "tracks reality" most closely carries a higher probability of minimizing unnecessary outlays of resources than does one made up of other kinds of beliefs. Furthermore, the near-universal esteem in which we hold "true," as opposed to "false," claims likely results from their having served our long-term survival as a species better than the alternatives. We may debate the philosophical merits of epistemological relativism all we want, but if our beliefs about the objective world, with its hazards and opportunities, are not roughly accurate, or accurate enough (more about that later), we are liable to make ineffective decisions and calculate risk even less fully than we do now.

Furthermore, many egregious human actions lie at the foot of false thinking. When the Bush administration launched a costly, protracted military campaign to depose the Saddam Hussein regime in Iraq in 2003 on the basis of what later turned out to be incorrect intelligence, with an ongoing monthly cost in the billions of dollars (not to mention the personal losses), it unwittingly created one of the clearest examples of the cost of false belief in modern history. Unfortunately, this history is littered with other such examples, starting with the terrorist attacks on 9/11 on the World Trade Center that set the stage for the invasion of Iraq in the first place. It was carried out, apparently, by individuals who were convinced that personal reward awaited them in an afterlife if they martyred themselves in a struggle with infidels against Islam. Such a rationale compares favorably with that behind almost every other major conflict in human history in which one side was convinced of the greater legitimacy of its claims or its moral superiority over the other. Historically, we have enslaved others or vanquished them to concentration camps because of their race or ethnicity, or aggressed against them because of their religion. In most of these cases, I would argue, false beliefs about the moral inferiority of the victims served as the principal justification. Of course, our actions at times may well be based on a careful analysis of the evidence, but, unfortunately, many times prejudice, bigotry, presumption, or impulsiveness passes for analytical thoroughness. The resulting false beliefs and the unintended consequences of holding them are both amplified when they serve as a basis for public policy.

This matter is complex, however, and its intricacies are beyond the scope of our treatment here. Suffice to say that more recent analyses of belief-fixing suggest that in at least some cases we make up our minds first and then collect information that supports our antecedent views, rather than proceeding from information to conclusion in a measured way. If so, then the quality of the information at our disposal has surprisingly little influence on what we believe about the world, and our argument here that corrupted information has a detrimental effect on correctness of beliefs is at least to some extent undermined. I think that the most defensible interpretation of this more recent research is to grant that our biases may to some extent filter what observations we think are true, but for most people most of the time they are not the chief determinant of our beliefs. If they were, each of us would hold an array of beliefs about the world that are independent of the evidence, and incoherent and contradictory, as well. We would be unable to agree on what evidence is telling us and be unmoved by logical argument. Surely such a world is not the one we currently inhabit.

Ripple Effects

To what extent does an individual's noncompliance with a particular moral norm affect the degree of compliance with it across the entire group? It seems to me that the degree to which members of a group in combination sympathize with complying with a norm suggests the metaphor of a vessel or *reservoir* of goodwill toward that norm, with each member contributing to or withdrawing from that aggregate quantity of goodwill according to his own degree of compliance. That is, each episode of compliance or violation increases or decreases the "contents" of the vessel by reinforcing or diminishing the overall sympathy for complying with it to whatever extent the episode affects others' actions. As a result, the future support for compliance with a particular norm may well depend on (1) the extent to which we all see the practical necessity for adhering to it, combined with, (2) the degree to which others, especially leaders and others in public view, are perceived to adhere to it, which encourages our own compliance. Two different dimensions of compliance are of interest here, namely, the *degree of visibility* of those who comply (or defect), and the *accumulated effect* of such actions on the aggregate embrace of the norm. While some of the argument here is speculative, recent scholarship supports the view that people's pro-social behavior can be calibrated to quite a fine degree by what they see.

Sometimes, defections from public norms of behavior are spectacular and become very public (the recent case of unethical and illegal accounting practices at Enron is an example). Mostly, however, compliance (or defection) consists of innumerable small acts by individuals, and their importance in generating or weakening support for a behavioral norm may be little appreciated. That is, they encourage observance of the norm through their symbolism, in that being seen adhering (or not) to the norm sets an example for others to follow. Robert Nozick argued (in *The Nature of Rationality,* 1993) just this point and suggested that our actions retain important functions (in standing for the principles we endorse) that lie beyond their more immediate function of satisfying our desires.

Our individual willingness to comply with a moral norm is doubtlessly influenced by many factors, not the least of which is probably the degree to which we think others are complying. Since we cannot know how willing everybody in the group is to comply, we have to rely for our assessment on the apparent willingness of particular individuals whose actions we witness. They, whether in person or through the media, become our role models, and consequently our willingness to comply with a norm may well turn at least in part (if not largely) on the degree of compliance we see from a visible subset of individuals around us.

While good, hard evidence that people in more public walks of life do play such a disproportionately larger role is elusive, it seems counterintuitive to argue the opposite—that the behavior of the most visible and "respected" among us has no greater impact on our own decisions about how we should act. Indeed, "respecting" another is tantamount to honoring what she values, and one way we honor those values is by emulating them. If we seek to emulate those individuals we most respect, how can the example set by such respected individuals not have a disproportionate contribution on group norms so long as there is some consensus about who the most respected individuals are?

As a result, some people may serve as more visible role models than others, and their actions have at least the potential to disproportionately influence others when it comes to fostering respect for a particular norm. Those of us, for example, who are in positions of visibility, such as teachers, clergy, media personalities, and, in particular, elected officials, may be under particular public scrutiny. The intensity of this scrutiny may be even greater for those who portray themselves (or are regarded) as having special moral authority or influence (because their defection from norm compliance might raise particular concerns about hypocrisy) or are expected to comply on account of their station within society.

Whether changes of norms in society actually originate from many small individual acts in a kind of "bottom-up" process or, contrarily, from a few more visible acts in a "top-down" model, or both equally, is unfortunately unclear from the research, and a thorough review of all the evidence for both views is unnecessary here anyway. In the end, instances of both kinds of change likely go on. Regardless, however, the focus here is on the accumulated impact of defections, and the assumption is that defections by more visible members of our society simply carry more weight in that regard. That is, it may be the case that acceptance of a particular norm rests in some delicate balance that can be upset by a small number of visible defections at one level or another. Perhaps an analogue is helpful here.

In atmospheric processes, a field with which I am professionally familiar, interactions across scales are abundant and ongoing. Perhaps the best-known recent expression of these interactions (in this case, from small to large) is found in what has come to be called "chaos theory," the view that small-scale events (such as the proverbial flapping of the wings of a butterfly) in one locale can effect larger-scale outcomes in remote regions elsewhere.

While whether such a particular kind of atmospheric event can have such far-ranging consequences has never actually been demonstrated, the example is a metaphor that illustrates how delicate various states of equilibriums may be, so that even very small perturbations may upset them and lead to the establishment of different steady states.

Do social equilibriums also exist that are equally sensitive to changes in maintenance structures? We do know that attitudes drift, that what was viewed as impermissible behavior in times past is today permitted. Indeed, our interpretation of religious texts seems to be continually on the move, and prohibitions on behavior two thousand years ago today seem seriously out of their times (consider biblical enjoinders against money changing, for example). How are these shifts brought about, and what is the role played by defections from the norm perpetrated by individual people in positions of high visibility? While we may lack hard evidence at this time that such shifts were specifically driven by "social" downscaling from a few prominent individuals to the collective, it is hard to imagine that specific, highly visible defections from a norm have no effect at any time on aggregate respect for that norm.

With an emphasis on the transfer of respect (or lack thereof) for an ethic (in this case, truthfulness) from the individual (particularly a highly influential one) to the group, the processes envisioned here are reminiscent of the "broken window theory" in urban sociology. In that theory, something as simple as a broken window, if left unrepaired, may encourage more general disorder and lawlessness. While the applicability of that theory, which has influenced urban policy for more than twenty years now, has been the subject of a spirited academic debate, recent research (*Science* 322, 21 November 2008, 1175) seems to confirm it, and it remains emblematic of the view that social states of affairs may hover in delicate equilibriums until nudged by seemingly inconsequential stimuli.

As members of a society, if we collectively hold some virtues as dear, we have an implicit understanding (in a contractual sense) with each other to help honor those values. If so, then the importance of our living up to this expectation is greatest *ceteris paribus* for those in high visibility roles because greater visibility may well be associated with greater potential to affect the reservoir of willingness to comply. In different words, with greater influence comes greater responsibility to uphold such virtues. If anyone is, those of us in high visibility roles are the literal "keepers of the ethic," which is why the behavior of our *public* officials is so critical to the maintenance of such norms.

Another form of possible "ripple effect" is the impact our growing disaffection with one particular moral norm might have on our commitment to other similar norms. The question is complex because it involves a lateral transfer of allegiance to one norm to others relevantly similar, and unknown factors may operate. Preliminarily, these may include how similar the norms appear to be and how strongly each is held. Despite the complexities, however, it is not unreasonable to suspect that such lateral transfers of commitment go on and that they wax and wane with time. We would expect, furthermore, our bundle of moral commitments to be an interrelated, coherent package rather than a disconnected set of contradictory individual principles; if so, then their coherence would suggest some degree of interdependence wherein allegiance to one affects the warmth of our embrace of (at least some) others. The point here is that additional unintended consequences may inhere in a disregard of basic moral norms that we generally esteem. In this case, not only would these consequences be unintended, they might well be little understood.

Finally, I think it is in the nature of virtue in general to be more easily undermined than shored up by individual actions. To illustrate with an extreme example, consider a society in which complete compliance with a particular norm is already the mean state of affairs. Continued observance of the norm only maintains the *status quo*, but any defections pull the societal mean below complete compliance. Particularly if they are defections among influential individuals, they may well have the greatest likelihood of diffusing to the wider population, further diluting aggregate willingness to observe. Of course, the assumption of 100 percent compliance is unrealistic, but the example illustrates how, unless some countervailing force(s) acts to continually reinforce moral commitment, the apparently inevitable fate of public virtue is one of erosion. If so, then a diluted commitment to one particular moral norm could have a very significant ripple effect on our willingness to observe others.

Economic Costs

The monetary costs of oversight measures put in place to detect and minimize all forms of ethical lapses in our society cannot be easily calculated, and it is even more difficult to isolate and identify just those costs associated with countering failures of truthfulness (as opposed to other moral/ethical lapses). Nonetheless, we can gain some appreciation for them by considering a few examples of such measures. For instance, various professional groups allocate resources to police the integrity of their own members, employing personnel to enforce and disseminate standards of behavior. We fund the Internal Revenue Service or state tax-collecting agencies so that they can maintain a vast infrastructure dedicated to preventing or detecting tax evasion. Laws are enacted and enforced (both requiring societal resources) concerning truthfulness in financial transactions at many levels in both the private and public sectors. Others are enacted (and must then be enforced by the judicial branch) that govern what firms may say in their advertising or promotional statements.

Other economic costs are less direct but perhaps much larger. America faces many public policy challenges in the twenty-first century, not the least of which are how to fund the rising cost of entitlement programs, growing domestic economic inequality, universal health care, global climate change, and formulation and application of an energy policy. The latter epitomizes many of the problems inherent in them all, with its wide cast of winners and losers and, consequently, the attention from various special interest groups. Each one vies for public sympathy with media messages slanted to make its particular case seem the most relevant and compelling; unfortunately, the truth may be a frequent casualty in this battle of messages, and the casual public is left with uncertainty about which point of view, if any, is the most enlightened. As a result, the voting public may fail to coalesce around candidates favoring any one particular program.

Conservatives will respond that government inaction is in fact the preferred state of affairs anyway and thus may welcome public policy paralysis. But many others of us decry the reliance solely on market forces that seemingly fail to provide adequate feedback before we find ourselves in one crisis or another. Arguably, failure to anticipate these crises reduces our ability to cope with them and increases their ultimate economic and social costs. For example, the sudden rise of energy prices through 2007 and especially 2008 had a dramatic effect on costs in many sectors of the economy, with the adverse effects spread widely across the society. Implementation of a broad national energy policy two decades or more ago following the last big run-up of oil prices, geared at the time to reduce our reliance on fossil fuels, especially petroleum, to reduce consumption overall, and to diversify our energy sources, would have spared many of us unnecessary pain from the current price spike. At the same time, it would have allowed us to avoid some of the unpleasant geopolitical entanglements in the Middle East in which we now find ourselves that threaten our national security.

The climate change controversy and very real possibility of runaway global warming is another policy area where government inaction has resulted in part from the conflicting messages of various interest groups, all hoping to influence the national debate in their favor. Of course, emphasizing only one side of a complex issue in order to produce an outcome favorable to your own interests represents one widespread form of untruthfulness (see following section); more egregious forms common in this debate consist of popularizing claims that are factually incorrect. All such strategies exploit normal scientific uncertainty and do not advance the quality or effectiveness of the national discourse insofar as solving important policy questions is concerned. If scientific projections are correct, the stakes in the climate change debate are enormous, with repercussions through many sectors of the biosphere, economy, and society. The more collective action is stymied and the longer we wait to address the buildup of carbon dioxide and other green-house gases in the atmosphere, the more serious the ultimate impact and the higher will be the remedial costs, according to current projections. In this sense, our inability to formulate an effective national policy in this regard amounts to a very real and growing cost that will likely be passed on to future generations. Our failure to muster the political will to act on the problem in a timely fashion is due largely to obfuscatory assertions by various interest groups that seek, with considerable success, to influence the outcome of the debate and undermine the public will for concerted action. We are left befuddled as an electorate, while the challenge mounts.

All in all, then, under examination the harmful consequences of untruthfulness in public discourse seems considerably broader and deeper than customarily recognized, and they are certainly not limited to just the damaged reputation of those engaging in it. Unfortunately, much of this damage is difficult to tally and thus evasive in measurement, which provides an opportunity for skeptics to deny its existence. Like global warming, assessing its footprint remains a scientific challenge, and there are those who want to see a strong scientific case that untruthfulness in the public arena is growing and has the wide toxic impacts claimed here before they are convinced that mitigating steps need be taken. How sure are we, they might ask, of the case before we commit additional resources to avert it? In this respect, as well, the consequences of public untruthfulness are like climate change, in that the costs are incremental and gradual, adding a stealth, almost occult, character to the problem that impairs our ability to recognize it before it is fully at hand. Inasmuch as a grasp of the magnitude of either problem is a social process, furthermore, it entails multiple variables in complex relationships that are only imperfectly understood; consequently, a hard, unassailable case on behalf of these harms is not in hand.

This difficulty does not mean that the best strategy is to deny and do nothing. The most convincing response to those who are skeptical of the harms being done by our tolerance of public untruthfulness is to point to the growing tally of regulatory steps (cited above) we seem to be taking to force honest, truthful behavior. I doubt these would be taken if a problem was not first perceived to exist. Fortunately for all of us, furthermore, when it comes to social trends or states of affairs, we do not need complete ("scientifically" solid) concurrence among the portfolio of evidence in order for mitigating action to be warranted. History reveals itself not by scientific sampling or experimental results but by a consensus of views. In this case, what is before us amounts to a credible account of the costs of untruthfulness that seem, in full, difficult to deny.

3 Why Truthfulness Challenges Us

If untruthfulness poses anywhere near the threat to our social fabric as I suggest, then why do we still engage in it, and why do we seem unable to accurately estimate the risks of doing so ahead of time?

The Ease of Untruthfulness

There are some characteristics about the nature of untruthfulness that make it seductively easy to commit and, as a result, one of the most common forms of (public) moral transgression (for lack of a better term). First off, being verbal, untruthful acts leave no physical imprint behind unless it is an electronic record. Absent such a record, detection is problematic, and it's easier to deny, perhaps making our commission of such acts less repugnant to us. Furthermore, because truth-telling has both ethical and epistemological dimensions, and we seem to hold the intent to tell an untruth to be worse than the act itself, the teller of un-truths can deflect questions about her motives by citing bad information or a misunderstanding on the part of the listener and thus avoid any disapproval by claiming that it was "an honest" mistake or that he was misunderstood.

Another reason untruthfulness is seductively easy to commit may be its incremental nature. Occasions of "spin," for example, can be very subtle and nuanced (and hence easy to deny); even a continuum of spin could be recognized from the slightest to the most bald, which makes very difficult the ironclad determination of whether someone is engaging in it. Other forms of moral failure, such as theft or assault, are more categorical; as an extreme example, one agent's action either results in the death of another or it does not, and while culpability for such a crime may exist along a continuum, the objective signature of the act is both physical and categorical.

A factor that further complicates disapproval of instances of exaggeration, spin, and outright prevarication is that these acts have an acceptable counterpart known as a "white lie," deception we might engage in to protect someone from learning harsher realities. I might encourage my daughter, if asked by a friend whether she is enjoying dinner at the friend's house when she is served a food she dislikes, to reply that she is "learning to like it." Of course, she isn't, but the feelings of her host are respected, and a greater good has arguably been served. Such behavior, of course, is generally encouraged and looked upon as being "polite," and we would probably regard someone who is bluntly honest regardless of the consequences as insensitive, at the minimum, or even rude.

Unfortunately, the very permissibility of white lying may set the stage for other more pernicious forms of prevarication because it's a small step from doing so to protect the feelings of others to doing so to protect oneself. In addition, one might feel justified in telling white lies not only to protect others' feelings but also to avoid feeling their disappointment or hurt (or even their anger) when they are confronted with unpleasant truths, a consideration that infuses white lying with self-interest from the start. Such a motivation is even more likely to be present when an exchange is between persons of unequal power or prestige, and the weaker individual feels compelled to tell the more powerful "what he/she wants to hear" out of fear or desire for approval. All in all, these considerations make the distinctions between various degrees of truth-telling messy at best, which in itself may do little to foster allegiance to an overall ethic of truthfulness.

Still another characteristic of untruthfulness that may make it easier to rationalize (and thus to commit) is that it can seem victimless, and as a result usual moral restraints may not apply. That is, we may be unable to see how it could impact the larger group. In fact, if the negative impacts are hidden or easily denied, the decision at the moment as to whether to be truthful or not may well be one-sided, particularly if the potential gains from telling an untruth are large (if it turns an election, for example) and thus difficult to resist.

Finally, in this electronic age, many forms of behavior are becoming more public than ever. Verbal utterances, however, are especially easy to disseminate because, at least by today's technology, they are by nature smaller electronic files than are visual records of behavior. Copies of what one says are much more easily circulated by the electronic media than are copies of what one does, and it has been thus for a long time. While with advances of technology both are easier to disseminate than ever, the advantage retained by the ease of transmission of spoken and written words is likely to be retained into the foreseeable future. Do these advances heighten the level of scrutiny of such acts or hasten their dissemination? The former might raise our awareness of them as violations of our cherished norms and thus discourage them. On the other hand, increasing the visibility of acts that in the past may not have been made public might also raise our tolerance of them, making them easier to commit in the future if they come to seem more acceptable. We shall have more to say about this matter later.

In summary, some distinctive features of untruthfulness give it the appearance of being a low-cost moral lapse. As such, moral sentiments, whatever they be, that might restrain us from such behavior are less likely to operate here than with more flagrant kinds of lapses. At the same time, all forms of communication (untruthful or otherwise) are more easily disseminated electronically in the public media than ever before, making what once might have been private utterances more likely to be public. Whether that increases their level of scrutiny (and hence disapproval) or their value as behavioral models (and hence approval) remains to be seen.

While these considerations show why untruthfulness might be thought of as an easy transgression to commit, or why doing so may be more visible than in times past, they do not in themselves explain what incentives or conditions account for our willingness to engage in it. What are some of these factors, and are any of them entrenched and accepted dimensions of modern society?

The General Incentive to Untruthfulness

Sometimes, the temptation to exaggerate, spin, or otherwise abuse the truth in discourse is so great as to be almost seductive in nature. Why is this so? At least two questions seem relevant here. First, is the character of these temptations to untruthfulness, whatever they are, similar to the pull each of us feels to violate our own moral principles in general from time to time, or are they specific to untruthfulness? Second, do these temptations inhere in our systemic social environment, or are they contingent, that is, unique and situational components of local events only?

The Imperative of the Present versus General Moral Adherence

I suggest that some of the incentive to untruthfulness is indeed common to all moral lapses and arises from what I call the "imperative of the present." Here is a sketch of what I mean. Taking into account the expected consequences of our actions (which is what adherence to moral norms requires of us) and then acting on that account often entails that we engage in some very special kinds of thinking that may be contrary to part of our nature. That is, compliance with moral norms sometimes requires us to put others' needs over our own, or to defer short-term individual gain for long-term group benefits, choices that run counter to our apparent predisposition to think and act on short-term rather than long-term consequences. Our preference for short-term response is not difficult to envision. In a competitive world with strong natural selection pressures, meeting immediate needs and threats must be a priority in order for any long-term existence (and replication of the species) to take place. More distant threats, while perhaps of great magnitude, cannot even be dealt with until immediate challenges are first met; a distant threat, furthermore, is not necessarily as likely to obtain as one outside your door (which is, hence, one of the rationales of that favorite maneuver by economists of discounting the value of things in the future). The present has an undeniably imperative quality for all living organisms because surviving it is required if replication of the species is to occur.

As a result, we (like other forms of life) face an array of "immediate" demands that are expressed (in us) as various (and often urgent) physical and psychological needs, and much of our behavior arises from the exigencies of these needs. Consequently, short-term needs often trump others, and responding to them is necessarily a large part of our total motivation. Consequently, we become fixated on the here and now rather than the somewhere, sometime. However, unlike all other forms of life (so far as we know), we remain capable of self-reflection, which includes envisioning future states, an ability that permits what we would characterize as "strategic planning" for the longer term, deferring expenditure of resources on immediate needs in order to preserve them for possible future use.

What emerges, then, is a picture of us as individuals who are frequently conflicted over short- versus long-term consequences. Pressured by our own biological needs and a survival mandate to focus on the immediate and individual, we are also endowed with the capacity to imagine alternative, longer-term outcomes, to calculate their probabilities and defer immediate pleasure for longer-term gain, and to understand how our local actions could have long-range implications for other members of the group. In other words, and very importantly, while at a deep level we remain tethered to the moment by our immediate biological needs, we are at least to some extent liberated from the yoke of the imperative of the present by our unique cognitive abilities. This line of thought suggests that the imperative of the present challenges all forms of moral reasoning, truthfulness among them. As a result, some of the incentive to be untruthful is clearly not specific to untruthfulness itself.

As an example, consider the case (profiled recently in the media) of a "conservative" Iranian newspaper editor who defined the role of his paper as that of "defending the Revolution," which meant that it often emphasized anti-American positions, even if that entailed falsely reporting certain news events. The editor evidently had decided that the short-term goal of defending the regime against doubt and criticism, thereby helping to assure its survival, was more compelling than any long-term commitment to truthful journalism (and, indirectly, the overall ethic of truthfulness) when the two goals conflicted. It is a clear clash of short-term versus long-term thinking.

The question then becomes one of determining how in each situation one should weigh global, long-term consequences against local/immediate imperatives, which becomes an ethical question when our answer impacts our treatment of others. We clearly have the potential to engage in long-term, global planning and to push our individual interests aside, which is what ethical choices ask of us, but what would *motivate* us to do so remains the challenge, and ethicists have long wrestled with the question, "Why be moral?"

Mustering moral behavior in general requires that at least two related prior conditions be met. First, we first need to understand how and to what degree our actions affect others (an empirical issue), and, second, we will need to *prefer* that our actions promote their good, or at least not cause them harm. We might, after all, be neutral on this question or actually prefer to harm them.

Assuming that not to be the case, our preference not to harm them would arise from a variety of motives that often crystallize from affective states. Two relevant ones are either feeling an emotional connection with them or holding an intellectualized sense that they have value of some sort, since if we hold them to be of value we will *want* to respect them; as we saw, *respecting them* is realized by either avoiding harming them or somehow enhancing their well-being. Many environmental questions, for example, boil down to whether we value future generations, the group most affected by today's practices (as in the continued buildup of greenhouse gases caused by unrestrained use of fossil fuels) sufficiently to take their welfare into account; some otherwise responsible people seem unconcerned about future generations when they endorse policies that disregard the impacts of status quo policies. Often, then, it comes down to a values issue that asks us to weigh immediate or individual gain against calculated (and frequently long-term) benefits to others.

Adherence to a moral code of behavior in general can be viewed as a kind of "public good," in that doing so benefits all; some people, meanwhile, may be tempted to "free ride" if the anticipated gains of defecting outweigh the costs, which are spread across the population. Though not the first to bring this particular strategic challenge to light, Garrett Hardin may have done more than anyone to popularize it within environmental science in his controversial paper "The Tragedy of the Commons." Originally written as a contribution to the then-current discussion on the challenges of human population growth, this paper argues for stiff population controls by maintaining that "commons," those dimensions of the environmental used by all but owned by no one, are inevitably abused just because individuals who initially take more than their share of the commons obtain significant benefit while costs of their abuse are spread thinly over the entire population. Market forces, that is, fail to provide sufficient feedback to the individual because user costs underprice the actual total value of the resource.

While Hardin limited his analysis to physically exploitable resources (such as grazing lands), many kinds of choices we make as individuals seem infected with the same type of asymmetry between individual gains and aggregate costs, and consequently the public goods issue seems applicable to a wide range of commodities (here construed in the very broadest sense). Accepted moral/ethical theory often specifies actions within a wide category of choices that disadvantage (in the short term) the individual, leaving him with a strong temptation to favor options promising greater individual gain that nonetheless comes at the expense of others. The benefits to us of exceeding the speed limit may be considerable (unless we get caught), while the costs to others are small, and an individual thief benefits from thieving so long as others refrain from it and absorb the costs of his individual behavior.

Thus, I think that the public goods issue highlighted by Hardin (which is a manifestation of the imperative of the present) is actually a far more common dimension in our ethical decision making than is commonly recognized. Compliance with moral/ethical norms in general challenges us just because the immediate gains associated with defecting can seem greater than the long-term costs (again, unless we get caught), and in this respect the calculus of adhering to norms of truthfulness is no different from adhering to other moral norms.

Some Incentives Specific to Untruthfulness

Beyond this knotty public goods/imperative of the present dimension that seems to reside in all questions about why we should be moral, additional extraneous factors seem to work specifically against the maintenance of an ethic of truthfulness in modern society, especially among our publicly elected officials. Identifying them now will help inform the subsequent discussion about what to do to address the overall problem. Seven major ones seem to be:

1. The Principle of Minimal Sufficiency

Whether the market corrodes or nurtures virtuous behavior has been long debated, with no clear resolution. Adam Smith was himself an ethicist and argued in *The Wealth of Nations* that repeated voluntary commercial dealings between individuals encouraged them to resist the temptation to engage in deception for a quick gain because of the damage done to their reputations. This thread has been explored by other champions of the market right up to the present. These observers argue that the market reinforces certain widely valued moral virtues such as truthfulness and self-restraint in those who participate in it. Because these virtues are also those important in civil society, these defenders of the market see it as having an overall positive social role to play.

Others, however, have long been critical of the atomizing, self-interest-promoting dimensions of the market. Contemporary criticism from the virtue ethicists has been particularly strong (MacIntyre 1984, 1988). Despite their cogency, I think that many of these critiques continue to underestimate the degree to which a market apparatus promotes deception by encouraging less than full-cost pricing. That is, because sellers are under competitive pressure to bring their merchandise to the market at the lowest price, they have little structural incentive for full disclosure other than reputation. In order for reputation to serve as a behavioral regulation, of course, feedback must be available to the consumer, and in some (perhaps many) sectors of the economy such feedback is lacking or too difficult to obtain. For example, we would have to go to great pains to obtain records from local repair shops or outcome data from neighborhood physicians but need both to make the best decisions as to which shop to patronize or which physician to seek out for a specific condition. Furthermore, both the shops and the physicians have incentive to keep such information from the consumer, perhaps even if their performance is exemplary, out of fear that it could be misused or not easily interpreted.

As a consequence, it is not a reach to suggest that the *structure* of the market relationship itself promotes deception and/or lack of full disclosure, and, while reputation concerns may have discouraged such practices in Adam Smith's day when transactions between buyers and sellers were often face-to-face and repeated, in today's complex economy the quality and availability of useful information about the performance of different sellers may be much more constraining. Anonymity, in other words, is more of a feature in today's market, and with anonymity comes a relaxation of the usual interpersonal forms of moral restraint.

Settling these counterclaims about the net influence of the market on our moral commitments, however, remains entangled in esoteric academic questions concerning the nature of the research, unfortunately. While the question is empirical, the answer remains very much a matter of debate.

Meanwhile, government regulation, a feature of our current "mixed economy" that is designed to address various market externalities, has long generated opposition from market defenders, who seem to ignore the observation that such regulation has *almost always followed* market abuses and failures. Examples to support such a claim abound, from the "robber baron" accusations (and legislative initiatives that may have resulted) of the late 1800s all the way to the comparatively recent passage of legislation such as the Clean Water Act. Such attempts to use government to reign in what are perceived as excesses of the market were/are reactions to antecedent market outcomes. Even now, the scandals that have recently swirled around investment banking practices (in 2008 and again in 2012) and the collapse of the subprime mortgage market in 2008 suggest to many that more (rather than less) regulation of that activity is in order, since the market in this area, if left on its own, seems unable to engage in adequate self-regulation.

Beyond all this debate, however, yet another important moral implication of market transactions has been largely missed. It is illustrated by the following fictionalized account:

One day, an old woodchopper was contemplating a particularly tough piece of firewood. "What," he asked, "is the optimal amount of force the swing of my split-ting maul needs to generate? Too easy of a swing will require a second or third blow with the maul, which wastes my energy. On the other hand, a swing harder than necessary wastes energy too. As in the story about Goldilocks, the energy generated has to be just right, or, in other words, *minimally sufficient* to the task."

What is minimally sufficient has to be just enough to meet the objectives, whatever they may be, and not a bit more. Why is this so? Why do we think in terms of what is minimally sufficient, in the first place? Obviously, constraints on the availability of resources play a major role here, as the old woodchopper did not have infinite energy to expend on this task. But why not? Why would he be ill-advised to expend all available energy on splitting one piece of wood? Second, how widely applicable is the principle of minimal sufficiency? Even a cursory examination, for example, suggests that it is a guiding princi-ple in evolution when a mutant adaptation arises within a particular evolutionary line that provides it *just enough* reproductive advantage to outlast its competitors.

In the face of competition, conservation of individual organism resources (to say nothing of safety) emerges as an important fact of survival and replication. No genetically based behavioral or structural adaptation need do anything more than provide a measure of reproduc-tive advantage in order for it to become more widespread in the general population. Evolutionary adaptation need not perfectly solve every chal-lenge of survival, but it does need to do so in a *minimally sufficient* way, one that confers some degree of advantage, and this advantage has to be just great enough to tilt reproductive rates in favor of the individual(s) within the wider population that possesses the adaptation.

And so it appears to be why, against a backdrop of constrained resources and the imperative to survive, minimally sufficient adaptations and thinking pervade so much of our own individual and group strategic calculation. It is, for example, at the heart of consequentialist ethical theories such as utilitarianism, in which actions are judged by their outcomes. The "right" action is the one that generates the best outcomes, however defined, *ceteris paribus*, and it need be only marginally better than its rivals in order to be preferred. As a result, while we may decide what to do based on some absolute standard, I think we are often more likely to do so by weighing expected outcomes and "satisficing."

Which brings us back to the market. For example, a firm need not offer the very best product, but it does need to be at least marginally better in some perceptible way than what is offered by the competition. With concerns about corporate bottom lines in a competitive market, firms have little incentive to engage in more research and development than is necessary to outdo the competition just enough to assure corporate survival and growth. Like the woodchopper who does not want to overswing, spending more resources than is needed for (sufficient) incremental gain would obviously be a suboptimal strategy. Indeed, the perspective of minimal sufficiency runs deep in the market. Even if a firm wishes to cultivate a reputation for going beyond what is seen as minimal, it enters a circular loop that, in a rational world, would prevent it from expending any more than the amount needed to cultivate such a reputation. In a deterministic world, constraining resources coupled with the imperative to live forces a symmetrical relationship between means and ends that dictates a conservative use of available resources that does not go beyond what is necessary to get by. In this regard, markets are, in effect, mimicking the larger outlines of biological evolution with their emphasis on minimally sufficient solutions.

It appears, then, that as marvelous as markets are at bringing order out of chaos without top-down regulation, they do have this perhaps unappreciated downside. That is, they may encourage an ethic of "just good enough" or "minimally sufficient" approach to things (just enough disclosure, or making a product "just better enough" than the competition) instead of "as good as you can."

However, would we approach morals this way (is "satisficing" an appropriate moral strategy)? Would we tell our children that they don't have to be honest, but "just honest enough" to avoid getting caught, or to be truthful only when being truthful can get them ahead? A morality that emphasizes opportunism is no morality, and an ethic appropriate for the market is inappropriate for our morality.

The issue is complex, however, because many forms of ethical consequentialism, as noted, require cost/benefit analyses that are tainted with hints of minimal sufficiency. Even the most rule-bound approaches require some sense of proportionality (or sufficiency) between a moral objective and the means to achieve it. By this view, refusing to help a mortally bleeding neighbor injured in an accident because I had already committed myself to meet a friend for coffee would constitute moral disproportionality (assuming that my overall goal is to follow rules that enhance the human condition in some way), in that I had avoided an opportunity to prevent great moral harm (death of my neighbor) in the pursuit of a trivial good; the benefit of keeping my commitment was less than the cost of doing so.

Because market economies are perhaps more prevalent and widespread today than at any time in modern history, the question as to whether market thinking is having an adverse impact on our commitment to related moral values seems especially urgent. While an answer in the affirmative does not require that we discard the market system or avoid answering questions of "should" with only economic calculations of costs and benefits, it does suggest that we may need to redouble our efforts to offset these effects, a topic we will discuss later.

2. Marketing/Advertising Practices and Strategies

Closely related to these concerns are those about marketing and advertising practices, which have long been the subject of moral analysis and critique. Some of that criticism has characterized the advertising function as little more than an amoral attempt to create wants in consumers where none existed before, which then increases consumption and materialism. This critique, in turn, has sparked recent interest in fostering greater morality in the whole enterprise, which (according to critics) has had only limited success.

Whether marketing and advertising practices encourage truthfulness through reputation concerns or have the opposite effect (both have been alleged) is not what I wish to address here, however. Rather, I want to review the more general *nature* of the relationship between buyer and seller and ask whether it *structurally* fosters misrepresentation. That is, because the advertised claims are provided (or funded) by the manufacturer of the products, the seller has a vested and legitimate interest in the success of the advertising, which fundamentally calls into question its objectivity and, ultimately, its truthfulness. It certainly seems clear that, in other venues, we are likely (and for good reason) to be skeptical of self-promoting efforts that are intended to provoke a response favorable to the agent engaging in it, and such skepticism appears appropriate in advertising, as well, even if there is disagreement about the exact extent of untruthfulness in advertising practices, overall. Certainly, we would not very strongly expect to get completely unvarnished accounts of the quality of product *A* from the merchant who represents and sells competing product *B*. As consumers, we are advised to cultivate a "buyer beware" attitude toward advertising claims, and the demand for truth in advertising has fostered the development of organizations such as Consumers Union, which provide independent information useful in sorting out reliable from unreliable claims. Of course, the existence of untruthfulness in advertising is not established beyond doubt by a mere perception that it exists, but the rise of such organizations signals at least a perceived need for reliable information untainted by self-interest. We assume here that this perception is at least to some degree anchored in objective reality.

3. The Rise of and Greater Reach of Parties that Willfully Distribute Biased Information

We owe to the postmodern movement in the humanities (and, to a lesser degree, the sciences) the recognition that even the most painstaking observations can be infected with theory and that even the most "objective" narrative has a particular point of view. Much has been said about this matter in recent decades, and the discussion continues to resonate, even in the sciences.

But such a recognition of accidental (and perhaps unavoidable) bias is not a license to infuse any account with as much bias as possible, particularly when it is being offered up as a truthful "objective" one. My reason for saying this is that we customarily trust each other to provide us accounts of things that are, as close as we can determine, certifiably truthful and not willfully exaggerated or distorted to serve undisclosed ends by influencing our opinions. We lack the time and resources to verify every assertion or claim that comes our way, particularly in this age of exploding amounts of information, and rely on the reputation for truthfulness that others cultivate.

Unfortunately, partisan sources of news and opinion seem to be gaining ground, and we consumers of information are often at a loss to distinguish objective reporting from bias. Agenda-driven research centers and "think tanks" release notes and commentary to the media, clouding public issues, and "talk radio" outlets push certain biases and distortion, or cherry-pick the news for sound bites or slanted reports masquerading as objectivity. To whatever degree the public is ill-equipped to detect and be skeptical of such bias in the media, these activities sow confusion and disinformation, and they probably do little to promote respect for truthfulness in the media or the public at large. Furthermore, growth of the electronic media has meant that more forms of expression can be transmitted faster to more people than ever before, increasing the reach of these activities.

To complicate matters further, interest groups with political agendas may seek to influence public debate by limiting the range of information available or to cultivate the impression of scientific uncertainty where little exists. Such groups can, and do, support the work of academic scientists through the awarding of grants on projects likely to shine favorable light on their agendas. Fossil-fuel consortia, for example, support scientific research that sows doubt and uncertainty in global warming projections because they may be losers in government-mandated changes in energy policy. Unfortunately, scientists who rely on such support to fund their research compromise their own objectivity when they feel obligated to generate results favorable to the interests of their funding agencies if they wish to receive future support. What scientist would literally want to cut off the funding hand that feeds her?

4. The Perks, Profits, and Status Associated with Elected Office

It probably goes without saying that, with so much reward (whether personal or financial) at stake, our political figures have very strong incentives to retain office as long as possible, and many respond by going to considerable length to do so. In such a context, the temptation for them to embellish accounts of their achievements and dismiss their failures to win voter approval is obviously very strong. Most people, even the strongest among us, will submit to temptation if it is attractive enough, and, when combined with the ease with which untruthful acts already can be committed, such temptation is even more difficult to resist. Indeed, given this combination, political office presents almost unique challenges to its occupants, at least when truthfulness is concerned. Many constituencies have dealt with the temptation for officeholders to go to such extremes to cultivate political longevity by imposing term limits. Unfortunately, such limits only remove the temptation rather than addressing the underlying proclivity to engage in untruthfulness in the first place.

For the sake of this discussion, of course, the important point is not merely that they are so tempted, but that, given their political stature, their untruthfulness is potentially so visible. While on one hand such visibility permits more scrutiny, which may dampen the impulse, on the other the damage done by untruthfulness in high places may go further to set a tone of acceptance of such acts than do instances of it in from less visible corners within our society.

5. The Ascendance of the Internet as a Communication Medium

Social interaction via the Internet offers participants an opportunity to avoid some of the usual restraints on face-to-face behavior. As a consequence, and particularly when communication can occur anonymously between individuals, it is no wonder that Internet conversation can be a more rough-and-tumble experience. Anonymity is a great leveler among participants of unequal power or expertise, but removing the usual restraints on antisocial expression also might unleash forms we would not otherwise expect in personal dialogue, such as untruthfulness and ad hominem attacks. The Internet is a double-edged sword in regard to truthfulness, because it permits rumor, hoax, and outright falsehoods to be circulated faster than in conventional social intercourse, but it also allows us to check the accuracy of information faster, as well. With a less-centralized flow of information in Internet communication has come a weakening of traditional journalistic oversight of the news, and as a result each of us becomes more responsible for checking the truth content of what we read online.

6. The Emergence of the 24-Hour News Cycle

What makes news is the anomaly, outlier, or unexpected. While commercialization of the media has always provided a reason for news outlets to focus on these dimensions of daily events, the incentive appears to be stronger with larger audiences and resulting revenue streams. The 24-hour cycle, meanwhile, increasingly fosters viewer ennui unless new excitement can be added. Some moves that generate excitement include spinning the news or selectively mining it for details that fit a preconceived narrative and add an emotional edge. Unfortunately, these same moves blur the distinction between news and entertainment when principled news reporting degenerates into dissemination of half-truths, or worse. What suffers, of course, is the ethic of truthfulness if it gets trampled in the competition for advertiser revenue and listener ratings. Moderation, compromise, middle-of-the road politics, and truthfulness are less interesting than extreme events or outlandish statements, which acquire a special allure, particularly in the all-news-all-the-time industry when the various media outlets are struggling for commercial survival.

One implication of these last two developments (No. 5 and No. 6) is a heightening of the importance of the individual not only as an author of decisions about what information to distribute and accept as true but also as a holder of personal responsibility at large. Interestingly, data suggest, in fact, that people who spend large amounts of time online tend to take a (libertarian) view of politics and social questions that emphasizes personal liberty and minimizes the role of government as an agent that can solve social problems. Whether this accentuation of unregulated individualism has been, or will be, accompanied by a growing rejection of group behavioral norms that have historically shaped our behavior remains to be seen, but it seems a short step to go from celebration of individuality to a more general rejection of such norms overall. I am not optimistic that those who are enamored of libertarianism will be swayed by arguments that appeal to the common good, as do those on behalf of truthfulness.

7. The Conviction that Ideological Ends Justify the Means

Finally, this condition rides the line separating causes of untruthfulness from forms of it. We will treat it here and revisit it again in the following sections.

Repeatedly throughout history we have seen examples when groups or individuals subjected (often "inferior") outsiders to forms of mistreatment or abuse that would be intolerable for members of their own group, and we need not recount them here. Alongside these examples prompted by moral discrimination, however, are other cases when we have concluded that an *abstract idea* (such as a cause or an ideology) justified taking whatever liberties were needed to advance it, as well. Of course, actions on behalf of religious causes come readily to mind, but partisan disagreements in the political arena often seem to take the same form. From the political right, for example, the rejection of actions to stem global climate change or generate new revenue, despite their rational appeal, may simply be fueled by concern that they run counter to the promotion of a small-government, low-tax philosophy. Advancing that vision, in other words, trumps adoption of what may turn out to be practical solutions to important problems and helps stymie compromise. In many ways, this practice resembles those described in sections 2 and 3, below.

Of course, a cause may indeed be so valuable that pursuing it swamps many lesser competing ones (in a life-or-death pursuit, for example), but whether advancing an *ideological* cause of this type does so first requires some kind of analysis and justification. The real failures here are in making the assumption that a *particular* ideological cause trumps the adoption of sound solutions that are in conflict with it, or in failing to lay out that justification in some rational form. Perhaps the usual absence of such an underlying justification signals that nothing convincing could be constructed along these lines.

4 The Many Forms of Untruthfulness

The Status of Truthfulness as a National Ethic

Why do consumer watchdog groups proliferate? Why do we need organizations such as Consumers Union, with net assets around $100 million, to evaluate products available in the market? Why is the oversight function in, say, the organic food industry, green construction practices, and various professions so robust? While most municipalities have enacted building codes that specify what kinds of construction practices are and are not acceptable, why do they nonetheless choose to maintain on their payrolls building inspectors to enforce these codes? The most generous among us might maintain that these functions serve only to preserve a standardized level of practice, but a more realistic interpretation may be that they are a crude metric of the degree to which truthfulness is a professed national ethic on the one hand, and the actual difficulty we have at living up to that ethic, particularly against the backdrop of a market economy, on the other.

Serious and reliable measures of truthfulness (and its trends) in practice are in short supply, unfortunately, despite the abundance of anecdotal evidence. Efforts to amass conclusive evidence are hampered by measurement issues (what exactly counts as evidence of truthfulness, or changes in the degree to which the virtue is respected?) and lack of an historical database. After all, who keeps a record of the number of times we each tell an untruth, even if we can agree on what exactly an untruth is?

But, as in the classic expression, absence of evidence is not necessarily evidence of absence, so we may infer some indirect indicators of a commitment to truthfulness (or lack thereof) by making two crucial assumptions. First, it seems legitimate to assume that provisions to enforce or encourage truthfulness are put in place because we perceive that such inducements are needed; that is, the inducements are a result of a perception of need. Second, we also may assume that such a perception is not entirely divorced from reality, so that what is perceived to be the case is at least to some extent a reflection of an objective state of affairs.

Granted these two premises, then, we can point to a growing list of practices around us that are designed to reinforce the ethic of truthfulness and at the same time stand as testimony to the degree to which we esteem it. These include but are not limited to (1) the lengthening list of laws being created by local, regional, and national legislative bodies to regulate individual and even group behavior that is related to truthfulness, and (2) the increasing use of codes of ethics to regulate or influence behavior in professional arenas. Many of these laws/regulations concern the practice of and need for full disclosure, obviously a truthfulness issue. For example, political figures or parties are increasingly required to disclose sources of campaign support, and lawmakers are being held to more explicit standards of conflicts of interest.

The Seven Deadly Forms of Untruthfulness in Public Discourse

It seems to me that the more pernicious or common species of untruthfulness group into certain familiar and distinctive forms, which I characterize below. Several of these may co-occur or reinforce each other, and the distinction between them is not always sharp. This typology is intended for illustrative purposes.

1. The Use of "Spin"

"Spin" is used here to denote the practice of including in a description of an event or an account of things only (or mainly) those details that are expected to benefit the describer or a cause s/he embraces. The objective, in other words, is to acquire a benefit rather than convey a truth, and for spin to occur the narrative being offered has to be selective. If outright distortion or falsification of facts is involved, however, while the practice is equally egregious it is not technically "spin," as understood here.

Spin is frequently on full display in political discourse. When in 2010 Massachusetts elected a Republican to finish out the term vacated by the late senator Edward Kennedy, partisans on the right claimed without exit poll data that the outcome was a stunning rejection of President Obama's legislative agenda (Kennedy was a Democrat and a supporter of that agenda). More liberal observers, meanwhile, in pointing out the lack of such polling data, lost no time in claiming that the election was evidently more about local matters that had little ideological/political implication. Both interpretations benefited their respective sides, but while promoting the liberal interpretation may have been, well, a bit tawdry, it wasn't an example of spin because it was based on an honest read of the absence of evidence. The view from the right, absent compelling evidence, was plainly an attempt to draw a highly selective read from the conflicting and weak data available at the time.

In another example, the problem of "climategate" in late 2009 was rife with spin. Hacked e-mails written by some prominent climate researchers suggested less than stellar scientific behavior on their part, which some on the political right (so-called "global warming deniers") then used to call into question the whole proposition of anthropogenic climate change. Briefly, based on a selective read of some references in the e-mails to the use of statistical shortcuts and the withholding of certain data from global warming skeptics, these skeptics were able to assemble a critique of the very heart of the case for global warming. While subsequent investigations revealed that none of the alleged transgressions undermined any of the fundamental details of the case, subsequent polls unfortunately suggested that this criticism of admittedly sometimes unsavory behavior by a few of the scientists involved in the research was successful in sowing doubt about the entire global warming problem. I think it is not too strong to assert that this skepticism was a direct result of the spin authored by a small cadre of critics who were less interested in an honest public discussion of this issue than in advancing their own political agenda and discrediting the legitimate work of others. Only time will tell whether public resolve in America was sufficiently undermined by this effort to stymie legislative initiatives to curb our growing greenhouse gas emissions.

Unfortunately, the use of spin is not limited to politicians but is common anywhere a public image is being cultivated, to wit:

Archaeologists have been excavating at the Old City site in Jerusalem for decades. With a long history of settlement and three of the world's major religions locally represented, this site continues to attract much public and professional interest. Not only do the findings shed general light on ancient life of the region, they also provide a particular opportunity for certain biblical claims to be tested, such as the existence of an ancient (tenth century BC) united and prosperous Israelite kingdom whose presence might bolster conservative Jewish claims to territory in the region. As a result, local parties are not disinterested in what is discovered or in how those discoveries are portrayed in public. Particular concerns have been raised over what is presented at the local visitor center, which is currently run by a nonprofit foundation whose members are mainly nationalist Orthodox Jews and whose goal is to promote Jewish settlement of the region. Obviously, they would have reason to be partial to some specific narratives concerning the results of the research. Meanwhile, others have suggested that in order to keep the presentations as objective as possible another (public) administrative arrangement should be sought.

I suspect that selectively omitting details unfavorable to us has been a part of our behavior almost as long as we have had self-awareness, and it may be one of the most widespread forms of untruthfulness in the public arena today. In fact, any conversation about public truthfulness is unlikely to get very far without venturing into the perceived behavior of political figures and their discourse, where exaggeration, embellishment, half-truths, and outright prevarication are thought to be so pervasive as to be the object of jokes. Voter participation in United

States elections currently runs about as low as it ever has, far lower than in most other Western democracies. Participation in presidential elections, for example, has declined from about 60 percent in the early 1960s to the lower-mid 50 percent range recently, and in nonpresidential election years it has fallen fully 10 percent during the same period (it was 37 percent in 2002). While percentages in Canada are about 10 percent higher than in the United States, the figures for both countries lag by substantial margins those from Europe, where average voter turnout for presidential elections generally runs 75 percent or more. Many factors undoubtedly contribute to this disparity, but the quality of the discourse and the reputation of political figures for spinning the news to their advantage are certainly factors unlikely to generate widespread voter enthusiasm wherever they appear to be prevalent.

2. Declaration of Unsupported Claims as True and a Rejection of Contrary Evidence Out of Fear of the Implications

This is sometimes called the *triumph of ideology over evidence* and leads us either to embrace "truths" that we hope or believe *ex ante* are true, or to reject well-supported claims (or arguments) because they sit uncomfortably with other beliefs we already cherish. At an individual level, it amounts to little more than a personal foible, but the matter is far more serious if it infects public discourse (see Chris Mooney's excellent account in *The Republican Attack on Science*). For example, many observers wonder why organized hostility toward the idea of evolution runs so deep in America, or why we often seem so eager to embrace such views as creationism in spite of a lack of empirical evidence on their behalf. Part of the hostility toward evolution seems to be a consequence of another poorly supported belief (particularly common among religious conservatives) that morality can come only from religious faith and that whatever undermines that faith (as Darwinian theory is sometimes alleged to do) will send us on a slippery slope to Gomorrah. As a result, many of this persuasion cannot bring themselves to accept as true what the objective evidence overwhelmingly suggests about our evolved past, much like the parent of the convicted felon who steadfastly maintains his innocence even in the face of seemingly undeniable evidence. Alternatively, they might accept "microevolution," the short-term response of biotic populations (such as viruses, bacteria, and insects) to natural selection but reject the suggestion that these responses, extended over great periods of time, can result in "macroevolution," wholesale changes in species' characteristics. This position permits them, for example, to recognize that insects or bacteria can develop (through evolution) more resistant forms but does not accommodate the possibility that wholesale changes in forms, such as the descent of early humans and great apes from a common ancestor, have occurred.

Some of the resistance to these ideas undoubtedly comes from an emotional basis. For someone long committed to creationism to suddenly accept an evolutionary perspective may well mean not only having to adjust other details of one's belief structure, but also to endure ostracism from other members of her community who might share her previous faith, resulting in a wrenching estrangement from family and friends. In such circumstances, discarding one view in favor of another amounts to far more than a mere change of views according to the strength of the scientific evidence (*Science* 2008).

Not all the examples of ideology or dogma trumping evidence come from the right, unfortunately. Questions about the notion of race have invited a divergent and passionate outpouring of opinions from not only academics but also other assorted observers (and was even the subject of a recent op-ed piece in the *New York Times*). While many biologists and medical specialists still maintain that racial groupings help explain patterns of susceptibility to some diseases or health conditions, other social scientists, especially on the political left, have abandoned the notion that "race" has any objective reality, viewing it instead as either a social construct or, at most, as resulting from biological responses associated with prejudicial practices. That is, unequal health risks or disease rates between racial/ethnic groups are seen as having more to do with stress, lack of opportunity, or access to health care associated with racial discrimination than with any fundamental race-based differences of biology. Those who hold this view sometimes find, even in the face of biological evidence, any discussion of "race" to be repugnant out of fear that it only adds legitimacy to racial discrimination. As a result, even what starts out as dispassionate scientific discourse around the notion of race is likely to become politically charged (witness the controversy surrounding the "Bell Curve," a book published in 1994 on the relative variation of intelligence in America, which many on the political left construed as having racist overtones).

Much in the same way, many social conservatives in particular are reluctant to embrace the emerging evidence that human sexual preference has a (perhaps dominant) genetic component that predisposes us toward homosexual or heterosexual behavior. Because they believe antecedently that we all have free will to choose how to behave and also that homosexual behavior is sinful, they are committed to the position that such behavior is freely chosen and that it is, therefore, a sign of moral failure. In spite of mounting research suggesting otherwise, they remain highly skeptical of such evidence, even when it is well-documented.

In still another arena, "vegans" who refuse to eat any animal products out of concern for animal welfare or the environment typically include honey on their list of unacceptable foods (since it is a product of an insect). Their justification for doing so is the claim that bees are harmed and exploited by beekeepers who may, for example, kill the entire colony to remove the annual honey crop or at least kill substantial numbers of bees when the colony is manipulated to remove frames of honey. In fact, killing the hive to harvest the honey is a practice followed generally only where winters are long and the value of the honey the bees would need to weather the long winter exceeds the cost of starting over with new bees in the spring. In all other geographic regions, the interests of the bees and the beekeeper are parallel and overlapping—whatever benefits the colony ultimately benefits the beekeeper, since it increases the odds of a larger honey crop. The beekeeper wants minimal losses of bees, with optimal colony health. Yet, among vegan circles this argument has little traction because it conflicts with other previously held views that using all animal products injures the animals involved, and honey, being an animal product, must have been obtained by harming the bees.

Finally and in a similar and now very familiar vein, during the run-up to the Iraq invasion of 2003, some in the Bush administration undoubtedly were convinced that Iraq harbored weapons of mass destruction irrespective of the intelligence reports. What was in question was not the strength of their conviction about this matter but, rather, the degree to which such beliefs were justified. Their acceptance of intelligence contrary to preconceived notions, which was apparently available but discredited, would have been inconvenient, to say the least, to their public position. Developing and executing national policy on the basis of doggedly held unjustified belief is a form of untruthfulness whose costs in this case have been both immense and tragic.

Most of us like to think that our beliefs cohere (fit together) in a logical narrative even if they do not, and some have pointed out that this form of self-deception is fairly widespread. On the face of it, limited receptiveness to new beliefs might seem justified if they challenge much of what we previously thought about the world, and each one requires a major reshuffling of our entire belief web in order for it to be accommodated. In this sense, resisting new and different beliefs in order to minimize cognitive dissonance with other existing beliefs also minimizes adjustment costs. Who, after all, would relish the thought of having to revamp every core belief we held every time we admitted one new one into our web of beliefs? Nonetheless, while minimizing such accommodation costs may be attractive from the individual's point of view, toting around an empirically unsupportable view of the world when we are called upon to make decisions that affect the lives of others raises profound ethical questions (more on this point later) and is a fundamentally untruthful stance.

3. Epistemological Absolutism (Often Associated with Religious Fundamentalism)

Closely related to the previous form, epistemological absolutism takes at least two slightly different forms. One can hold onto a particular version of truth by believing that it, and it alone, will always be correct, even if that belief is fundamentally testable and revisable. In this case, one is choosing not to do any evaluation/testing/examination of the cherished belief. Absent contrary evidence, of course, holding on to a demonstrably true belief is what rationality would dictate, but, at the same time, unwavering allegiance to one view can close our minds to other possibilities and in the face of contrary evidence reduce us to the realm of the dogmatic.

If I may be allowed a slight digression here, I would observe that exactly what counts as an adequate justification for a belief or a warrant for action has been another point of debilitating disagreement among epistemologists that I wish to avoid in this commentary. In doing so, however, I am not maintaining that all justifications are necessarily of equal, or no, value (which then might imply that we are justified in believing whatever we wish, come what may). Clearly, in the history of human thought, some ideas (consider scientific theories, for example) have displaced others on account of their perceived evidential support (and here I reject the relativistic claims by sociologists of science that such theory replacement amounts to no more than the social interplay within scientific communities and has nothing to do with questions about their goodness of fit with greater, more credible evidence). In addition, a little personal introspection on each of our parts would probably show us how we each have changed our minds about things when presented with new evidence, suggesting that in practice evidential support and confirmation do indeed play a role in shaping our views of our world.

Epistemological absolutism is also present when we display a dogged adherence to untestable claims about the objective world. Without examination and testability (or, after Popper, falsifiability), of course, we cannot know when/whether our beliefs are wrong, and hence cannot be sure about them until they are somehow tested; it may have been "revealed" to me that certain human traits, such as dark skin, are associated with certain kinds of undesirable behavior, but a rational, unbiased person would not put stock in such a view until it was subjected to some level of scrutiny.

Anyway, the debate over use of embryonic stem cells for research is an example of this form of epistemological fundamentalism, in that whether fetal cells are biological tissue or living entities is a central but untestable issue; given the lack of scientific evidence for the latter position, viewing such cells as equivalent to human life, as opponents of embryonic stem cell research do, is little more than a retreat to a religious judgment about an empirical state of affairs. As with all such judgments, the question then becomes, is it correct? Unfortunately, because such views are matters of faith rather than reason, they are immune to rational scrutiny, and without such scrutiny their truthfulness is indeterminable.

In some such cases, we can become so certain of the correctness of our beliefs that even extreme strategies they generate seem justified. In other words, and with a nod to Machiavelli, the end then justifies any means necessary. History is replete with examples. Those in the Nixon administration implicated in the Watergate break-in apparently believed that America was under siege by disloyal antiwar elements and that unlawful behavior was fully justified in order to save the country from their further influence. Flying planes into skyscrapers and killing thousands of innocent people in order to advance a particular religious interpretation is another example. Even America's invasion of Iraq, carried out amid questionable intelligence but under the conviction that it nevertheless posed a genuine national security threat, is emblematic.

Without going into unnecessary philosophical contortions here, we need to distinguish between a determined adherence to a course of action stemming from a well-justified belief, and extremism, which I associate with courses of action or strength of belief out of proportion to either their costs or the supporting evidence. What counts as adequate justification for a belief is a matter of long debate among epistemologists, and along that line I offer nothing to further that discussion here. I think, however, that we can and routinely do distinguish degrees of confirmation between views that are better supported by available evidence and those that are not. On the extreme end, unfortunately, we find those whose strength of conviction overreaches the strength of the evidence, or even cases in which conviction is disconnected from scrutiny of any kind.

For example, on the evening of 19 November, 2005, in Haditha, Iraq, a unit of American Marines reacted to the detonation of a road-side bomb by killing twenty-four civilians, including ten women and two children, in a tragic event that was later to be investigated as a possible war crimes incident (and not fully resolved until 2012). How these Marines rationalized such an act at the time was at the heart of the investigation. One of the concerns was that, rather than acting out of self-defense in the heat of battle, these soldiers had dispatched the civilians in order to send a message to the local residents about the costs of cooperating with the enemy, and civilian lives were expendable merely as a "cost of doing business" in pursuit of the mission. More specifically, it was alleged that such an attitude about the expendability of civilians in general, their diminished value in comparison to the value of the overall mission, was widespread in the ranks of the military at the time.

There is little doubt that some form of this view must pervade the thinking of soldiers nearly everywhere, or else the commission of acts of war would become morally impossible. In war we must be *certain enough* about the importance of our mission that, if necessary, we can justify (and hence morally accept) loss of human life in its pursuit. Such certitude, in other words, allows us to overcome our moral repugnance toward acts of war and violence. While it might be justified in cases of sheer self-defense, when, for example, we must take another life to save our own, being so certain of the correctness of our actions in other less urgent circumstances that we still feel justified in taking *any actions whatsoever* has historically led to the loss of countless lives. We need look no further than the Crusades, the Inquisition, or the killing fields of Cambodia for examples of the cost of epistemological fundamentalism. More will be said about this issue as it relates to religious belief (and resulting behavior) in a later section.

4. Hypocrisy

Hypocrisy is a kind of nonverbal untruthfulness that consists of the commission of acts inconsistent with espoused principles. The recent goings-on in the Dover, Pennsylvania, school district over what may be taught as "science" provide one illustration of the issue. With a vote of the school board in October 2004, the Dover school district became possibly the first in the country to mandate the teaching of "intelligent design," which holds that the universe is so complex it could not have arisen by chance alone, in its ninth-grade science classes. This move triggered a legal challenge on behalf of a coalition of parents and other interested parties that was presided over by Judge John Jones. In his verdict, delivered on 20 December, 2005, Judge Jones ruled that a public school district in Pennsylvania cannot teach "intelligent design" as a part of a science curriculum. Tucked into his decision was the following observation (see *Natural History*, June 2007, "Darwin in Court," by Richard Milner, 28–32):

> It is ironic that several of these individuals [intelligent design advocates], who so staunchly and proudly touted their religious convictions in public, would time and again lie to cover their tracks and disguise their real purpose.

This observation captures what seems to be the essential problem here—saying one thing and then doing another, and sometimes we seem to fixate on finding examples of it in the behavior of our national figures. It is not hard to find in the political arena. Some recent examples include an administration calling for Americans to accept sacrifices for the war in Iraq while they themselves have to make few such sacrifices, and several influential conservative religious and political leaders who have publicly condemned homosexuality or opposed equality legislation subsequently having their private gay lives exposed.

5. Three Fallacies that Often Pass for Sound Argument

Matters of justification and warrant, touched on above, are never far from our discourse. In the public sphere, for example, different parties with contrasting perspectives often disagree about what problems should be addressed or whose claims should be first served. While the challenges facing us are already complex and laced with uncertainty, the question of what to do about them becomes even more muddled when fallacies are passed off as sound reasoning, and segments of the public are confused as a result. The problem is that fallacies are customarily (and properly) employed in debate, in which one wants to "score points" and defeat the arguments of an opponent, but such stratagems are inappropriate for discourse in the public square where the goals are to share information and perspectives and formulate informed policy (rather than defeating the arguments of opponents).

Nonetheless, fallacies appear in public discourse very frequently and assume many forms, but three seem to be especially common. The first of these is the *fallacy of the excluded middle*, the portrayal of controversies as consisting of only extreme views ("you're either with us or against us in the war on terror"). In reality, one can imagine many intermediate and nuanced positions between these two extremes, and to exclude this broad middle ground or pretend it does not exist raises questions of truthfulness.

The second one is the use of *straw-man* arguments, in which opposition views are distorted or mischaracterized in order to make them easier to attack and discredit (a particularly powerful debater's move). Those in favor of the war in Iraq often characterized their opponents as unpatriotic, which reframed the debate from one about the wisdom of the war to one about which view (support for or opposition to the war) was most patriotic. In so doing, such an argument had the effect of suppressing dissent and marginalizing the war critics, who felt they were expressing patriotism in their own way. In another example, religious creationists have often disparaged evolutionary theory, which concerns the development of life, as denying a role for a "creator" in the origin of life and, hence, of "fostering atheism." Darwinian theory has nothing to say about life's origins, and it is a straw-man argument to say that it does.

The third common kind of fallacy is the *posthoc argument*, wherein sequence is incorrectly interpreted as evidence of causation. The 1950s were a decade of unusual weather extremes in the United States, with several exceptionally hot, dry summers that rivaled the historic dry years in the 1930s. At the same time, the military was engaged in extensive above-ground nuclear weapons testing, and it did not take long for some observers to attempt to causally link the two; soon almost every extreme meteorological event was claimed to stem from "atomic testing." With a longer and more detailed set of climatic records and a better understanding of atmospheric processes, we now see that such extremes had physical causes within the earth-atmosphere system and that tests of such weaponry had little to do with them.

5 Addressing the Problem

Intrinsic and Extrinsic Motivation

Before getting to the specifics in this section, I would like to reflect on the general issue of individual behavioral regulation. Perhaps arguably, particularly when it involves anger management, it is one of the greatest challenges we collectively face. The question is simply this: by what approach or method will we achieve the highest level of compliance with group behavioral norms? Certainly, fear of direct retaliation by others serves as an important constraint on some of our actions (as in game theory) when we are not anonymous or when we have repeated interactions with the same party, or parties, even if we are. But many ethical questions involve onetime interactions between individuals unknown to each other or even, in the case of environmental questions, with nonhuman entities that are incapable of reciprocating. In these sorts of cases, when fears of reprisal are irrelevant and thus unlikely to provoke us to regulate our own behavior, what other incentives to self-regulation might be at work or could be invoked?

Fortunately, there remain other incentives, both intrinsic and extrinsic in nature. We are motivated *intrinsically* to do something when we do it primarily for the good feeling we get afterward, for the satisfaction of achievement or feeling of accomplishment. We might help a stranger in need not out of any expectation of material reward, perhaps even putting ourselves at risk, but simply because we felt it was the right thing to do at the time. Quite possibly we were prompted by empathy for the stranger's plight and acted on an emotional rather than rational level, an example of what is commonly viewed as altruism.

On the other hand, *extrinsic* motivation would spur actions (or discourage them) out of an expectation that something will happen *to* us (not *within* us). As noted above, fear of retaliation is one common kind of extrinsic motivation, but many others are equally common. Complying with a speed limit to avoid a traffic fine or completing an act out of an expectation of a monetary reward would both be examples of extrinsically motivated behavior. I might do something for you under the expectation that in relevantly similar circumstances you will do the same for me, or give you a gift on the assumption that sometime in the future one will be forthcoming from you. In a capitalistic economy, perhaps the most glaring example of extrinsic motivation is the "profit motive," which prompts exchanges with others expressly for personal gain.

In general, psychologists have long advised against sole reliance on extrinsic forms of motivation to achieve compliance with important social norms, particularly in education, where students accustomed to getting gold stars or stuffed animals for achievement soon come to focus on the reward itself rather than deriving pleasure from the act of learning. Economists, on the other hand, disagree, and their view seems to be gaining ground in educational circles, where paying students for achieving learning objectives is becoming more common.

For the purposes of this discussion, we can assume that both kinds of motivation involve incentives but that one (extrinsic) is rooted in conditions external to ourselves. While those often assume a material form (we do something to get a *thing*), the motivation can also arise from the content of a verbal transaction, as when we do something under the expectation of praise. Although in some cases more than one kind of motivation may be in play (we can likely all remember instances of our doing things not only for pay but also for the satisfaction of seeing them done), my purpose in this discussion is to distinguish those cases in which mostly intrinsic motives dominate from those in which extrinsic ones prevail.

While, as might be expected in social science, not everybody accepts such a distinction in the first place, framing the issue in these terms seems to put matters into stark, and more digestible, terms useful for the subsequent discussion here. Fortunately, much has already been written about both this topic and the implications of the existence of intrinsic motives, particularly from the viewpoint of education, and we need not revisit the surrounding and sometimes fierce debate it has engendered (see Alfie Kohn's *Punished by Rewards* for one popular and enduring treatment of the virtues of intrinsic behavior in the classroom).

Obviously, as a society we resort to both forms of incentives to elicit group behavior consistent with the kind of society we jointly want and expect. Laws and regulations are common examples of extrinsic motivation encoded to reduce the incidence of what is seen as defective behavior. At the same time, we seek to instill a sense of ethical responsibility in our children at home and in our schools. Encouraging them to "do the right thing" clearly appeals to their inner conscience, a matter of intrinsic motivation.

While achieving the kind of society I assume we want is possible through reliance on either form of incentive, doing so through intrinsic incentives has distinct advantages associated with smaller transaction costs. Creating and maintaining structures that generate extrinsic motivation not only erodes our freedoms but diverts resources away from other endeavors, which creates sizable opportunity costs. As Kohn and others have pointed out, any increase of behavioral regulation through extrinsic means requires more legislative micromanagement of our lives (laws governing areas of behavior) coupled with heightened surveillance and policing and a growth of the judicial system, all to keep undesirable behavior in check. More police and/or judicial infrastructure would be needed, as well as more legal experts willing and able to handle the increased amount of litigation. If conservatives object to what they see as the unnecessarily heavy judicial burden we now bear as a society (including the purported overabundance of much-maligned "trial lawyers"), the prospect of still more litigation to reign in the behavior of a larger number of citizens unwilling to be trusted on their own to abide by laws and regulations should unsettle them even more.

Suffice to say, in such a society we would all end up paying more either in the form of higher taxes or as user fees levied at the time we utilize whatever government service we need, or both. These fees could be disguised as higher court costs, legal costs (for attorneys to defend ourselves against hostile litigation or to initiate litigation against others who are transgressing against us), or user surcharges for certain explicit government services. As was recently (March 23, 2010) observed in a *New York Times* column, "Moral Lessons, Down Aisle 9," "markets don't work very efficiently if everyone acts selfishly. You end up with high transaction costs because you have to have all these precautions to cover every loophole."

Then, of course, there is the opportunity cost of greater policing and/or judicial activity. Either option would obviously consume resources that could be better spent elsewhere. In an antitax political environment where revenue enhancement is politically difficult, every dollar spent on these ends is one not available for other worthy programs, and even libertarians agree that government has some legitimate functions to perform that require financial resources. Unless public agencies resort to user assessments at every stage, or other forms of revenue enhancement can be found (such as through casino licenses, etc.), additional enforcement responsibilities would have to come out of general funds, which might jeopardize education expenditures, support for emergency responders, or support for public welfare programs (such as the arts). In a finite budgetary "pie," rising expenditures in one area quickly ripple through the entire enterprise, with disturbing implications for other areas of expenditures.

In addition, we have the unmeasurable harm done to the morale of the citizenry by both growing regulation and higher costs of living. How would we react in the face of continually higher taxes imposed because fewer people could be trusted to comply with the law without the threat of penalty? In the absence of enhanced revenue, what would be our reaction to the assessment of more user fees every time we encountered a government service? How would we feel about augmented surveillance, police, and security presence in ever increasing areas of our personal lives? Finally, reliance on extrinsic motivation to prompt compliance with social norms runs the risk of both discouraging behavior we want when a reward does not appear to be forthcoming and encouraging behavior we do not want when no one is looking. I doubt that we would look favorably on a child who tells her parents that she will "be good only if you reward me."

Greater reliance on intrinsic motivation avoids these costs and complications and leaves resources free for the pursuit of other ends. Unfortunately, the advantages of such a strategy escape many observers. Conservatives extol the virtues of the market and abhor government regulation, but they fail to acknowledge the many significant ways that our participation in a market may undermine our intrinsic motivations, as we saw earlier. While defenders of the market strongly dispute this claim and assert that virtues such as trustworthiness, self-control, and a sense of fairness are all nurtured by participation in a market system, their defense is questionable. It misses the important question about the degree to which markets nurture extrinsic, rather than intrinsic, motivation, which is central to our consideration here if indeed intrinsic motivation is associated with less cost compared to extrinsic motivation.

Whether such an assumption is true is a question without a well-supported answer either way, unfortunately, and in its absence we will for now fall back on what seems intuitively evident. That is, participation in the market reinforces just those virtues needed for successful participation in the market, and only to a minimally sufficient degree. In other words, in a market we need to *appear* to be trustworthy and fair in our market relationships, and only when doing so is in our best interests. With the central emphasis on doing things for personal material gain, the market tilts the ledger toward extrinsic motives, because the perspective it seems to instill in us is an expectation of exchanges and external rewards that runs counter to the notion of doing something out of personal pride or because it is right. Furthermore, rather than encouraging us to do the best we can, we are incentivized to do just enough to get what we want.

As we noted earlier, this may be a good way to approach decisions about how we should allocate our resources, but it is an inferior ethical approach. Random acts of unrewarded kindness or acts of self-sacrificing altruism, behavior we associate with intrinsic motivation, would seem disincentivized in such an environment. Ethical behavior requires us to sometimes forego personal gain for principle or the welfare of others, whereas in the market personal gain becomes *the* principle.

Curiously, an implication of this analysis is that conservative political parties that simultaneously favor small government (with little regulatory role), reliance on the market to allocate as many goods and services as possible, and strong moral commitment ("family values") are embracing a hopelessly contradictory agenda. That is, if market psychology undermines intrinsic motivation, and we continue to marketize more dimensions of our lives, more of the work of behavior regulation will have to be done by extrinsic motivation, which ultimately entails more regulation and oversight. Advocates of small government and market solutions to problems cannot have it both ways.

Nonetheless, and against this rather bleak assessment, I agree with its advocates who say that market approaches are here to stay as a core feature of many political/economic solutions. My primary reason for saying so is that, in a long meta-view, the system that appears to work best for nation-states will be chosen by its own consequences in a version of natural selection, that is, in the market for social/economic systems, and there is something deeply counterintuitive about the notion of a market for ideas leading to a preference for a nonmarket type of political economy. In addition, recent political history has seen the preference for free market systems strengthening. Certainly during the late twentieth century, with the collapse of a planned economy in the former Soviet Union and its satellites, and economic liberalization introduced in China, market systems became more prevalent than their rivals, and that trend gives us every reason to believe it will continue.

Consequently, and reluctantly, I conclude that we need to learn to live with whatever long-term corrosive effects on our ethics that market environments might turn out to have by neutralizing them whenever possible. In the context of this discussion, that means either promoting settings that nurture habits of truthfulness intrinsically or altering the set of extrinsic motivations we face so that the articulation of truth and truthfulness is more strongly elicited than its alternatives.

To that end, I offer a set of prescriptions intended either to offset extrinsic incentives that appear to undermine our respect for and commitment to public truthfulness or to enhance intrinsic motivation to be truthful by identifying several modest (and relatively low-cost) adjustments and initiatives within our reach. Overall, the prescription is a bit like that for global warming: even with some scientific uncertainty about how much of the warming is due to natural causes and how much is anthropogenic, diversifying our energy portfolio and reducing our overall energy use are good things to do regardless of what the exact cause of the problem turns out to be. And so it is with these steps that might offset the temptations to untruthfulness.

Some Specific Suggestions

1. Maintain Public Vigilance

I start with a very low-cost move. We may have heard it said that "when people know better, they will do better," an aphorism that suggests that at least some ethically deficient behavior occurs because we are unaware of how our actions adversely impact others. In our case, we may not recognize that what we do involves a form of untruthfulness, or we may consider it a harmless violation of a norm. If so, we have no incentive to do otherwise.

In the case of public untruthfulness, a good first step might consist of the relatively simple task of enhancing the public's awareness of the issue, which means drawing attention not only to incidents of untruthfulness in the public sphere but also to the more subtle costs of it vis-à-vis the undermining of trust. Letters to editors of newspapers and contributions to other forms of public discourse (such as blogs) all have the potential to enhance awareness of both the problem and its impact on trust. Fact-checking services need to be supported and their results disseminated as widely as possible.

2. Increase the Availability of Public Research Money to Academia

Academia is unlikely ever to have all the resources it deems sufficient to support all the research it deems necessary to carry out, but as a society we could be more generous than we currently are. Stronger research support has many societal benefits. While it is likely to provide long-term payback in the form of findings that better inform public policy debates about the many technical issues facing us, such as global climate change, the more immediate benefits include stronger support for legitimate science and scientists in general. When public support for research is stable or shrinking, college faculty, under mounting pressure from their institutions to publish, have growing incentive to look for research support under almost every proverbial overturned stone, which increases the attractiveness of agenda-driven sources that in better times might be shunned. Increases in the amount of public research support would lessen the degree to which scientists are tempted to turn to these questionable private funding sources (as in the case of global climate research being funded by fossil-fuel consortia). Fortunately, in a competitive enterprise such as scientific research, good money available in sufficient quantity may drive out bad, given the stigma among scientists often associated with accepting funding from sources with questionable agendas. The problem associated with accepting support from politicized sources, of course, is that pressure from the source for certain kinds of results may compromise the objectivity of research being funded, particularly if the likelihood of grant renewal is contingent on the nature of past investigative results. In addition, stronger public funding is more likely to attract better scientists to the domestic scene and may stimulate something of a reverse "brain drain" that helps attract (or retain) skilled scientists to America. In short, upping the public support for research has many benefits, both short and long term, not the least of them being the diminishment of the lure of biased bucks.

3. Maintain a Free, Open, and Independent Press

A free and open press permits scrutiny of statements made in the public domain, raising awareness of the issue and thus helping to regulate it. News media not beholden to the political leanings of editorial oversight are absolutely essential in this endeavor; unfortunately, the independence of the news media in this country is currently being challenged by a wave of corporate mergers and takeovers, as radio stations and newspapers are being increasingly consolidated under only a few major companies. In and of itself, such consolidation does not necessarily threaten journalistic independence of news outlets, which provides critical oversight, but it does indeed increase the opportunity for politicization of the process.

Offsetting the corporatization of the media requires that independent sources of news and commentary be vigorously supported either by the government or private donors. Congressional wrangling over funding of and leadership at NPR/PBS led by conservatives during the administration of George W. Bush only underscored the importance of such public support and the necessity of its remaining unconnected to the political content of the products aired. At the same time, the virtue of the individual donor cannot be diminished: while corporate donations to public broadcasting could provide important revenue, any one corporate source, as well, may be tied too strongly to particular program content, which reduces journalistic independence. The current reality seems to be that, as government support for public broadcasting continues to dry up, whether from fiscal limitations or policy squabbles in the legislative arena, a mix of funding sources increasingly centered around corporate and private donors will likely be needed.

Unfortunately, while such a "user pays" approach may bring approval from conservatives, it may not bring the even-handed, non-partisan coverage of the news we citizens of a democracy necessarily need. Because users of the media generally prefer to hear perspectives expressed that they antecedently agree with, support for such media would most likely come from self-selected segments of the listening audience. Outlets consistently voicing conservative opinions are more likely to attract conservative listeners, which in turn would further support the expression of conservative points of view. Other media identified with more liberal viewpoints are more likely to be supported by more liberal listeners (the alleged but objectively unsubstantiated "liberal bias" of PBS, for example, is well known among conservative circles). A result of this self-selection is a kind of "balkanization" of the media, with different segments of the audience tuning into and supporting different outlets rather than all listening to the same source expressing a mix of viewpoints.

This trend has not escaped the attention of critics. For example, in a recent (March 19, 2009) column on just this topic in the *New York Times*, Nicholas Kristoff summarized research suggesting that Americans are increasingly segregating themselves into like-minded communities, at least insofar as our voting behavior is concerned. Such a trend matters because it could mean that we are becoming more polarized and intolerant in our views on social issues.

If so, the important overall point here is that preserving an independent and impartial segment of the electronic media where all points of view are aired is important to national interests, and, like our public schools, it should to be nurtured and supported with public funds. Doing so provides the greatest assurance that it would remain independent and serve as a stage for the marketplace of ideas. This goal could be accomplished by establishing a line item for its support in the federal budget that is not subject to negotiation each year. Meanwhile, although politicization of oversight is always a threat, journalistic impartiality of any such federally supported medium could be overseen by an independent body.

A media-scape in which such a source is replaced by a constellation of outlets, each pushing its own bias, with listeners tuning in to find what they want to hear, would appeal to those who argue that more choice is better, but according to recent evidence we have good reason to suspect that it would instead have the unintended consequence of further isolating individual listeners from diverse opinions that they need to hear to be better informed but wish not to hear. The irony would be that promoting choice (one way of enhancing individual freedom) in this way would not likely promote the aggregate good if it led to more voter isolation and division.

The role of blogs on the Internet as one more source of news and opinion remains unclear in this regard. Certainly, thorough and objective reporting of events and investigative exposes can be found on the Internet, but the problem is a lack of journalistic oversight of the products. As a result, the objectivity of blogs varies widely, and it is a caveat emptor environment for the public. Distinguishing verified reports and substantiated claims from hearsay and biased opinion requires effort, time, and a skeptical eye. Even assuming availability of resources, however, many users may not be as critical or skeptical as the medium requires, and a willingness to accept all Internet information as reliable all too often results in the diffusion of rumor and false reports.

A root issue here is the degree to which we are each personally willing to accept unverified information as true, a subject about which I have more to say in a subsequent section. In the meantime, if we are to learn to be more skeptical, more constructively critical of what we encounter in the public media, our schools seem to be one place where such critical skills could be emphasized.

4. Include Critical Thinking Skills in the School Curriculum

The emphasis given to critical thinking skills in our schools has long been a point of debate, with different views unfortunately reflecting the "culture war" between conservatives and liberals across the wider society. Mostly, critical thinking, however defined, has been less warmly embraced by conservatives, who favor traditional education objectives. Such a preference, meanwhile, has not stopped others from pushing for greater inclusion of the teaching of such skills in our schools (for example, see the Foundation for Critical Thinking).

In the education arena, progress in especially two areas would be helpful. First would be more training in logic and thinking so that we are better able to engage in logically correct inference and recognize faulty thinking, including fallacies, when we encounter it. Second, beyond training in such methods, however, I think we need to nurture a greater appreciation of the value of evidence-based decision making and being seen as doing so, and of not overreaching evidence or being afraid of saying, "I don't know" when necessary. Obviously, such a stance requires that we recognize that, if the history of human inquiry has taught us anything, it is that our understanding of the world is, at best, tentative, provisional, and revisable.

A companion objective stemming from this observation would be to nourish healthy (positive) skepticism, which is not synonymous with nihilism, particularly in our schools. The emphasis would be on encouraging students to raise a reasonable amount of doubt about easy answers to complex problems, or to probe further into solutions that seem obvious but are untested. The benefit of nurturing such intellectual habits is that gullibility can kill if it leads us to substitute ineffectual problem-solving strategies for legitimate ones; at a minimum, gullibility leaves us personally vulnerable to swindle and scam, no small risk in this age of electronic crime and identity theft (Pigliucci 2009).

Of course, the enhancement of critical thinking skills and skeptical habits would have little benefit if we lacked a sufficient understanding of the issues to analyze them intelligently in the first place, and our willingness to follow current events obviously influences both our knowledge of them and the degree to which our votes reflect this knowledge. Unfortunately, research suggests that most voters are little informed of current issues. Voter apathy and ignorance have attracted abundant comment from across the political spectrum, with the right, for example, claiming that it shows a need for smaller, less complicated government, while those on the left call for measures to improve voter literacy. Some despair at having any impact on the problem and are content to let our democracy limp along as is.

I argue that some tweaking is both possible and desirable and that our schools and homes are suitable places to start, with a greater emphasis on keeping up with current events. In schools, the initiative could include more formal incorporation of news in the classroom from sources known to be relatively impartial, or an examination of different news sources known to be biased in different directions. Granted that, in this era of educational testing and objectives, teachers have less discretionary time in their classes for such exercises than they used to, incorporating a current events theme in a portion of at least some classes is still only a matter of deciding that it is important to do so. At home, making available hard-copy news periodicals is easier than ever, given the shrinking use of such outlets in favor of the Internet and the resulting availability of discounted subscriptions as media firms attempt to recapture some of the lost market. At the same time, conscientious parents might want to continue to go to lengths at home to discuss events currently in the news with their children.

We are all busy, with finite resources to address what seem to be growing demands on our time, and we all prioritize as a consequence. Amid it all, keeping up with current events and instilling the importance of doing so in our children is one of many choices we can make about how to use our time wisely.

5. Nurture a Broader Self-Interest Conception in Our Society

The values, assumptions, and perceptions we each bring to options facing us help determine what choices we make, including whether and to what degree we adhere to specific moral principles. Slowly, we are coming to understand just how complex our decision-making processes can be, as revealed by a lively agenda of research now being carried out in the behavioral and neural sciences. Gone seems to be the standard image of us as nothing more than self-interested rational calculators in the traditional image of *Homo economicus*. Instead, the emerging picture is that in some settings we are guided mainly by emotion or intuition, in others by standard rational calculation, and in still others by values and perspectives inherited from our culture or immediate environment in a complex interplay that can sometimes frustrate scientific attempts to render the motives fully intelligible.

However this inquiry turns out, one element in this mix of decision-making approaches of interest to us here is the extent to which our own stylized view of "costs" and "benefits" shapes our decisions when we approach choices analytically. This question of how we assess costs and benefits is especially important to ethicists who subscribe to an objective, consequentialist (the goodness of acts is measured by their effect rather than their intent) view of ethics like utilitarianism, which holds that choices about right and wrong should be based on rational calculation rather than on subjective preferences. It is also, of course, absolutely integral to neoclassical economic theory, which assumes that we are each little more than "utility maximizers."

Certainly, in consequentialist ethical systems, which, arguably, are much in favor among Western philosophers, there is tension between the idea of "costs" and "benefits," and we find an array of viewpoints about how wide one's circle of mindfulness ought to be when they are being calculated (for example, see Singer 2000). This disagreement extends into the popular culture, as well. For example, when, during the 1980 presidential campaign, Ronald Reagan famously asked the voters whether they were better off than they had been four years earlier, he identified a point of view with which many in the electorate could relate. It was a view that contrasted sharply with that which underlay JFK's prescription to "ask not what the country can do for you, but what you can do for your country." The Reagan view situated the measure of quality of political outcomes mainly in our own *individual*, lived-in experiences, whereas the Kennedy view nested it much more solidly in the welfare of the *collective*.

These two extreme views harken back to distinctions we earlier drew between short-term, self-interest-dominated thinking heavily influenced by what we called the "imperative of the present" and other kinds of analyses more focused on long-term, large-scale consequences. Both viewpoints, and hybrid versions between the extremes, seem to be present in the population at large at any one time, as noted in earlier comments. Some of us, for example, might spend more to buy a product because we think it is "greener" than a competitor's, while a neighbor is uninterested in this distinction and buys only according to the price on the shelf.

This discussion only underlines how profoundly our own definition of "self-interest" affects the choices we make and how, I argue, implementing a narrowed version often generates additional costs later. Controversial legislative initiatives in Congress, for example, may be more likely to win support when measures are included that specifically benefit the individual districts of wavering congressional members, even though such measures increase the overall cost of the final legislation. With an eye on the best interests of the wider collective, those legislators would not need to be prompted with narrowly targeted features designed, ultimately, to enhance their reelection chances, and the resources of the collective would be respected, but absent such a focus on the well-being of the collective, a legislator would be more likely to see it through a "What's in it for me?" lens.

Despite the overwhelming evidence that different conceptions of self-interest sometimes drastically affect the way we make choices, many questions about this issue remain. For example, we do not know exactly whether our preference for one or another form of self-interest conception is genetic or environmentally rooted. Recent research suggests that at least some components of it may have a genetic basis, while social environments (such as parental influence) are also important.

Regardless of its roots, however, what I want to consider here is (1) whether evidence suggests that the breadth of our self-interest conceptions is relatively stable or is situational and, (2) even if it is basically stable, whether over the long term it still responds to some degree to changes in our social environment.

Regarding the first question, if we each bring a fresh version of our self-interest conception to every new choice situation, then how widely we look to assess our costs and benefits when we are attempting to be rational calculators should vary each time. That is, sometimes we might take into chief account very broad impacts and at other times very narrow ones, generating low overall predictability to our behavior. If, however, we each follow a characteristic pattern of looking either more broadly or narrowly at the consequences of our choices, then the net impact of our particular self-interest conception would be more strongly expressed over the long term and be of greater interest in this discussion. While strong experimental evidence favoring one interpretation or the other remains elusive, observational evidence suggests that individuals are likely to follow a consistent pattern through time in the determination of the outer limits of their self-interests. Such personal differences among us are likely to be expressed in a range of choice settings we face and may even help explain why some of us are consistently more congenial toward egalitarian public policies, for example, than others are.

As a consequence, then, how as adults we come to define our particular self-interest conceptions emerges as an important question for us. Doubtlessly, the traditional views of both "nature" and "nurture" have roles to play in this determination. If, however, it turns out that the predominant origin is traceable back to genetic influences, then such patterns might traditionally have been seen as locked into place and beyond environmental modification. Recent research indeed seems to be confirming the existence of some genetic control over such behavior but at the same time is finding that social information can lead to changes in the brain and behavior through effects on the genome itself. That is, not only is the matter more complex than we earlier thought, but a more important role for socialization in the development of such preferences seems to be emerging from this research.

If so, the question then comes down to the nature and extent of the role played by the "nurture" of social environments. For example, do the structure and form of the discourse about what we should do and value encourage or discourage us to think in particular ways about this question? Ronald Reagan's famous question, by locating the value of public policy (as practiced by the federal government at the time) solely within the realm of the individual, was an attempt to skew the discussion in one particular direction that resonated strongly enough with the electorate, apparently, to help turn the election away from Jimmy Carter. The intriguing general question is whether (and to what extent) similar moves affect the longer-term discourse and, in this instance, have lasting impact on the way we think about our interests more generally.

There is serious reason to think that attitudes that determine how we interpret just what is in (and out of) our self-interest are at least partly derived from the environment in which we make such choices. In other words, the discourse, practices, and institutions of the culture in which we live can, in the extreme, affect our willingness to embrace either wider or narrower conceptions of self-interest. Much could be said, for example, about the geographic patterns of voting across America, with conservative politics being the norm across certain regions such as the Great Plains. If we associate conservative politics with public policy that emphasizes individualism rather than collectivism, the conservatism of the rural Plains represents a coordinated expression of one particular (in this case, narrow) self-image conception, which is nurtured and repeated within the region by shared attitudes, institutions, and practices. The null argument, that such influences or overt expectations have no impact on us, requires us to reject the role of "nurture" in setting our values and attitudes and to look elsewhere to explain broad geographic patterns of voting, a view that is simply contrary to the accumulated wisdom in social science. Regional patterns of behavior such as this one strongly suggest causes that operate above the level of the individual.

As humans, we engage in political activity out of a conviction that the future can be better than the present and that we individually can influence the course of events. The identification of factors in social settings that contribute to our behavior raises the distinct possibility that these factors, and hence their effect on our behavior, are alterable, that our own "nurture" is a candidate for intervention by the agents being nurtured. If so, should we attempt to do so, in which direction, and why? My short answer is yes, and in the direction of more far-reaching considerations because customarily taking the longer-term view seems most compatible with adherence to moral principles such as truthfulness.

Ethics comes down to a struggle for human behavior that is founded on a widened conception of self-interest out of a consensus that better outcomes obtain than when it is not. If not, why, with "golden rules" and codes of ethics, would we devote so much time and energy to encouraging ourselves to think of others? Furthermore, because adherence to moral principles frequently requires self-denying choices from each of us, and because the rationale for that self-denial is frequently articulated as arguments about the welfare of the collective ultimately benefiting the individual, broadly defined self-interest conceptions would seem almost by definition to be more friendly to the observance of moral norms than would narrowly defined ones. Put another way, what we might characterize as "enlightened" self-interest is more likely to lead to compliance with moral norms than would narrower forms, all things considered.

If we desire compliance with moral norms because it leads to a more well-regulated, ordered society, and if we prefer to meet this objective wherever possible through reliance on intrinsic rather than extrinsic motivation, then we have good reason to try to promote broader conceptions of self-interest when we can do so. The goal is lofty, but we can accomplish it largely, I believe, through grassroots efforts in our schools, communities, families, and especially in public discourse that, taken together, prompt slow, incremental change rather than trying to tackle the problem with broad, top-down revisionism. In sum, we would be seeking to effect a gradual reconceptualization of our self-interests in our own hearts and minds.

The approach I recommend is based on the assumption (which is consistent with suggestions from recent research in this area) that how we think and talk about such things affects how we think and talk about them—that we get from people pretty much what we signal we expect from them. If so, we can tweak the feedback loop with a bit of personal effort and vigilance. In this case, discussions about what we ought to do that we hold with family, friends, and members of our community can be infused with gentle questions about, among other things, "who benefits?" because doing so often helps focus attention on making choices that serve the widest possible audience no matter at what level the discussion is taking place. Of course, this question situates the motive for actions, including public policies, in benefits to people (as opposed to, say, the environment), but answering it may require us to consider impacts on a wider circle of others ("wider" both in terms of our immediate circle as well as future generations) than we might otherwise. Not only are such questions as "who benefits?" and "what if everybody did that?" useful to pose to our children when we are talking with them about what they should do in their everyday lives, but they are also a useful lens through which to think about group policies, whether at the family, community, or national/international level.

As an example, let us consider what two different wage earners might do with their discretionary income (that which is left after financial necessities are covered) under different conceptions of self-interest. Both of them wish that their expenditures bring them some form of personal satisfaction (pleasure, utility, happiness) but, in addition, the second one, in conjunction with an awareness that different choices affect different groups of people, is actively seeking to have wider impacts with hers. The first one, consequently, decides to spend the surplus on a luxury cruise, home entertainment center, or sports car, whereas the second diverts it to support public radio, invests it in household renewable energy systems (such as a small wind turbine or photovoltaic system), or contributes to a charity that supports microloans for third world agricultural development. To the question "who benefits?" both would reply that their investments are returned to the economy and help generate employment, but they do not all necessarily serve the same breadth of objectives, because the expenditures of the second party contribute to the common good in a way that those of the first party are unlikely to. That is, the second party has helped underwrite a listener-supported public good or has invested in technology that addresses the joint concerns of energy independence and global climate change. It is not a leap to conclude that the second wage earner has invested her resources more wisely because the potential benefits are spread over a wider circle of impacted individuals. The collective itself has benefited.

The point here is to illustrate how different decisions we make (which depend on the values and assumptions we antecedently hold) about what to do, such as whether to buy or live "green" or adhere to the ethic of truthfulness, can lead to remarkably different outcomes. Not only do those values and assumptions help originate our preference to do one thing or another, they themselves appear to respond to how we think and talk about them in a two-way relationship. The subtle but still remarkable conclusion is that we have some agency in determining what goes on around us that leads us to see the world in various ways. If our environment is eliciting and encouraging mostly short-term, individualistic self-interest calculations, and if we believe that better outcomes would be associated with broader self-interest conceptions, we have it in our power, through education and modifications in the way we engage in discussions of our choices, to alter our social environment and, ultimately, the outcomes of our choices.

6 Religion and Its Limits

Reflecting on the challenge of reinserting an ethic of truthfulness into the public sphere reminds us, unfortunately, that no consideration of moral instruction, inculcation, or reaffirmation in America today could proceed without some reference to religion, which is widely regarded as an integral part of moral instruction. Few qualities of our political leaders are subject to as much scrutiny as is their religious affiliation and activity. For example, in the 2008 campaign, we remember that the media took the further step of becoming fixated not only on our presidential candidates themselves, but also on religious figures associated with them, as though their views would be transmitted in some uncritical way directly into the candidates' heads and become virtually the only moral compass each had. Of course, few Americans would want amoral leaders, but linking their religious views with their morality raises serious and even troubling questions. Even when for the first time in our country's history we stood on the cusp of nominating either an African American or a woman to be a major-party candidate for president in the 2008 election, the odds that an avowed atheist or agnostic could be similarly nominated remained vanishingly small, all

75

the while in several other Western countries political figures disavowing religious affiliations of any kind are increasingly visible and embraced.

As a result of such deeply held religious values in America today, there seems to be a widespread conviction that morality could not exist without religion. Many would argue, after all, that we humans are inspired by religious faith to great works of good, and to good behavior in general. A recent (2006) effort by Worldwatch Institute, for example, argues just such a case (i.e., that religion has been and could continue to be a strong positive force in the environmental movement). Social conservatives are especially likely to conclude that remedying morally deficient behavior (such as untruthfulness) would require incorporating more religious training into the lives of our children, thus increasing (in their view) the likelihood that they will grow into morally responsible adults.

Unfortunately, we have plenty of reasons to think that these ideas are mistaken. First off, not only have important steps in social justice or welfare been initiated throughout American history by secular leaders (Jacoby 2004), but currently we see conspicuous examples of avowedly secular figures spearheading humanitarian campaigns or underwriting their costs. These examples call into serious question claims about the linkage between religiosity and morality. Second, the use of religion itself to implement adherence to a moral code raises several philosophical and practical issues that are difficult if not impossible to ignore. The following extended discussion highlights some of these.

Meanwhile, I readily acknowledge that the following discussion may seem to be a digression from the thrust of this book up to this point, but I feared that any conversation about rectifying a moral dimension of our aggregate behavior would seem to be missing something if it did not include a nod to religion. Of course, I take issue with that view and hope to show why in what follows.

1. The Motivational Problem

One of the principal problems with using religion to motivate certain behaviors among its adherents is that doing so may be counterproductive. Any religion that inspires allegiance through the promise of unverifiable rewards (such as spending an eternity in the company of loved ones or with numerous pulchritudinous virgins) is trading in matters of extrinsic rewards and therefore represents just another form of market transactions where we do things just because we expect to be rewarded for them. As we saw earlier, such an approach collapses ethical decisions into the more usual market-situated prudential ones and robs us of motivation to be moral when the incentive, for whatever reason, is removed. While one may argue that ethics prompted solely out of enlightened self-interest (in this case, out of a desire to receive the promised rewards) is better than no ethics at all, such an argument is inadequate because it fails to show that, all things considered, we are better off relying on extrinsic rewards than on any rival system. So far as I am aware, such a case has not been made. If we prefer, instead, to rely on enhanced intrinsic motivation to offset the negative influences of the market, as discussed earlier, implementing a set of extrinsic incentives to promote behavioral regulation is inconsistent with that goal.

A heavier emphasis on intrinsic motivation leads us away from conceiving human interactions as little more than market transactions and permits a fuller embrace of altruism as a legitimate human motive worth enhancing. Altruism, in turn, is understood as arising from what virtue ethicists (after Aristotle) would refer to as "good character" and is associated less with the usual calculations of individual gain than with certain character attributes and habits.

Of course, some deny the existence of altruism in humans altogether and argue that underlying even the most clear examples of self-sacrificing actions still lie calculations of self-interest. As a result, they see an embrace of extrinsic motivation (such as the notion of rewards and retribution in an afterlife) as a means to promote moral behavior to be fully appropriate and consistent with their view of humans as always prompted to act by prudential calculation (and never altruism). In other words, because these skeptics believe that psychological egoism motivates all other similar kinds of calculations, they advocate such motivation as a means to attain future compliance with desirable norms and are untroubled by the use of such incentives in religious contexts.

Several details about this overall view are unsettling. First, it represents what Scottish philosopher David Hume identified as the "is-ought" problem of justifying moral norms from empirical states. That is, according to Hume, deriving statements about what we *should* do from what currently *is* the case raises serious logical problems. While not all philosophers agree with Hume on this point, many do. Second, it is based on the faulty argument that all acts of (intrinsically motivated) altruism only appear to be altruistic because of our inability to get to the bottom of the behavior; according to this argument, were we able to do so, with more thorough psychological analysis, for example, we would inevitably find evidence of egoism, which would vitiate the supposed altruistic motives that prompted the act in question. With such a rebuttal at hand, skeptics of the existence of altruistic acts are always ready to dismiss them. Rather like the childhood claim that a ghost is in the closet, and any skeptic who fails to see it is not looking hard enough or at the right time, this claim about altruism is logically irrefutable. That is, as with irrefutable claims in general, if no observation logically exists that could refute it, it is untestable (and of course could not ever be considered either true or false as a result). Antialtruists are invoking a fallacy to defend their view (in this case). It may be that research into cognition and motivation will eventually shed light on these questions, but until such time we will stand on the view that to whatever extent religious belief extrinsically incentivizes actions it diminishes whatever role is left for intrinsic motivation, an outcome that is counterproductive in the long run if we agree that, all things considered, intrinsic motivations carry lower transaction costs.

2. Epistemological Problems

Other objections to using religion in pursuit of these ends center on how religious beliefs are acquired and the risks associated with acquiring any beliefs in such fashion. Because religious doctrine frequently has serious logical and philosophical weaknesses, the mere act of embracing it often requires that usual limits of credulity be bypassed or ignored. In other words, we are asked to accept on very limited or nonexistent evidence claims that in other venues we would be likely to reject by virtue of their sheer improbability. For example, the tenets of most monotheistic religions in general hold not only that deities intervene in earthly outcomes but that they regularly do so as a result of imprecations (in the form of prayers) from us.

Yet, such a belief is based on a number of faulty assumptions. First, praying for a different outcome implicitly suggests that we are dissatisfied with the expected one and have a "better" scheme in mind. But such an assumption contradicts our view of a deity as being omniscient (a usual quality attributed to him/her by believers). How could fallible humans purport to have an understanding of things that is in some way superior to that of a (putatively) omniscient god? Second, in order for us to know whether any such prayer has been answered, we would need to be able to discern answered prayers from lucky breaks or unanswered prayers, a nearly impossible task (one might say that, at very least, it is "epistemologically challenging"). What criteria could we use to make such a distinction? The few serious investigations into the effects of intercessory prayer in medical science have shown little or no evidence that it helps in the prognosis of those for whom the prayers are offered. Confirming a positive, objectively expressed impact of such prayers in our personal lives, with no scientific control and limited observations, seems virtually impossible.

Yet, contrary to the evidence, such beliefs widely persist. We look at low-probability outcomes in our own lives, such as avoidance of an accident or recovery from low medical odds, and conclude that they could not have happened without intervention, and we cling to such beliefs even while others around us suffer similarly low probability (but negative) outcomes in spite of their own prayers. Our belief-forming mechanisms, unfortunately, are poor at calculating the probability of such outcomes, and we are generally predisposed to interpret events around us according to our antecedent beliefs even in the face of strong contrary evidence, especially if the beliefs are otherwise attractive to us.

Further examples demonstrate how inept probability calculations infect the evolution-creationism debate. Creationists and supporters of "intelligent design" are critical of evolutionary theory because it posits a low-probability (and thus counterintuitive) mechanistic origin for the development of complex life forms. Yet, the three mainstream monotheisms themselves postulate even lower-probability solutions for our origins:

The human species exists on a minor planet on the edge of the Milky Way. Our galaxy has an estimated 400 billion stars, countless planets, and enormous clouds of gas. The spiral arms of the Milky Way extend some 50,000 light-years, revolve every 220 million years, and speed through space at 400,000 kilometers per hour heading toward our nearest galaxy, Andromeda, with which it appears to be on a collision course. There are billions of additional galaxies overlain with stars. *Can it be that all this was designed with the human species in mind* (emphasis added) (Kurtz 2009)?

According to literal Christian teachings, for example, a supreme being responsible for bringing all of it into existence created only humans in its image and accorded only them (one species amid more than a million now known and perhaps three to four million all told on earth) special status. Not only is such a claim wildly counterintuitive in a statistical sense given the size of the universe, it raises other questions about why, of all species, we should warrant such special status and treatment in the first place. Answering this question by invoking anthropocentric religious views that supposedly establish the surpassing value of human life on earth, in turn, creates logical difficulties akin to the fallacy of begging the question, in that scriptural authority is used to resolve a question about scriptural veracity.

On the other hand, some may argue that different truths are involved in religious beliefs. We might, for example, recognize not only empirical truths (those tested against observation), but also spiritual (those that come to us in flashes of insight, or revelation) and logical truths, which originate from rules of logic or even mathematical relationships. Because of this diversity of truths, it is argued, we should not expect that religious truths should necessarily stand up to empirical testing.

The danger of such an approach is that we end up with a smorgasbord of different beliefs that have passed different kinds and degrees of test, and we are pulled toward both methodological schizophrenia and relativism/subjectivism. When beliefs conflict, which one is more likely to be true, and how would we know? If multiple epistemologies are all thought to equally converge on the truth, we are left with incoherent beliefs when the results conflict. Sadly, the notion of "different kinds" of truth that are all equally true cannot be disentangled without some form of test, and for that we seem obligated to rely on observation; if so, empirical truths are logically prior to all the others. If not, the result is that every belief is equally justified, and, hence, equally acceptable as a basis of action. Chaos results.

Absent an all-things-considered method for evaluating rival truth claims regardless of their source, what is the purpose of belief in the first place? I believe it is error to conclude that the purpose of belief is to satisfy one's psychological needs, because one who so concludes ends up believing not what is most likely certifiably true, but what is desired to be true, in a form of wish fulfillment. In such a world, I am free to decide what car to buy based on the best available evidence, but I am also free to hold other beliefs absent empirical support, for example that people of colored skin have lower moral worth than others. I think it is only a short step from believing claims about transcendental existence and divine influence in our lives without evidence to believing the worst about people in the face of a similar absence of evidence.

Teaching Tolerance, published by the Southern Poverty Law Center, recently reported a curricular experiment in one California school district that sought to promote religious tolerance among its students by offering a course about the diversity of contemporary religious faith. Evaluation of the impact of the course on student attitudes afterward revealed an increase of tolerance for beliefs different from their own, certainly a laudable result. School officials were also pleased to note that few students reported any change in their basic religious philosophy (in other words, that their original faith had been left intact after their encounter with new religious ideas), which was one of the initial concerns of the families of the students enrolled.

While parents who want their children to hold certain kinds of religious beliefs rather than others might be gratified by such a result, it also speaks volumes about the nature of our religious belief in general, for it shows how rigid we normally are about such matters. We hold them very deeply, and normally regard them as immune to rational critique. What some may see as having a "strong faith" unshakable in the face of adversity may amount to little more than a stubborn refusal to consider alternatives: would we not honestly want to know whether what we believe is as strongly supported as what others of different views believe? A classroom of differing religious views is a microcosm of the world, in that each resolutely believes her views to be preferable to every other mutually exclusive set of beliefs. While we want to celebrate an atmosphere of tolerance and respect of such diversity, it is logically impossible that all such (often contradictory) views are equally well supported and likely to be true, and when foundational beliefs conflict so, too, should we expect that behavior conflicts.

3. Belief and Behavior

In spite of the degree to which religious belief systems raise such grave and debilitating epistemological difficulties, however, the center-piece of my critique of religious faith as a preferred route to morality focuses mostly on the lack of empirical evidence that it works. We see very little reputable evidence that holders of faith-based value systems behave any differently from the rest of us, unfortunately. Obviously, absent such evidence, religious faith loses its luster as a panacea for enhancing the strength of moral norms such as truthfulness.

First, let us consider the question as to whether holding religious beliefs is associated with some measure of moral behavior. Considerable social science research has demonstrated little difference between the behavior of those who characterize themselves as religious and those who do not, at least in terms of easily measurable key attributes, and anecdotal evidence is no stronger. In 2009 alone, for example, we witnessed two prominent Republicans, South Carolina governor Mark Sanford and Nevada senator John Ensign publicly confess their marital infidelity; both represent the party of conservative religion and "family values," and Sanford, in particular, was outspoken about former president Bill Clinton's indiscretions when he was in office. Not only does such anecdotal evidence continue to raise questions about the connection between public displays of religion and personal behavior, aggregate social indices suggest that countries with higher percentages of people identifying themselves as nonbelievers often score higher on measures of social well-being. Zukerman (2006) goes so far as to claim that "the most secular countries—those with the highest proportion of atheists and agnostics—are among the most stable, peaceful, free, wealthy, and healthy societies." While care is needed to avoid concluding cause and effect here, it appears from the data that religiosity does not automatically lead to more civil society. In fact, some evidence suggests the reverse may be true.

Second, consider the interesting but difficult question regarding both the positive and negative influence of religious belief on human history. Debate about this question has long simmered, with one side pointing to contributions by believers while the other objects by citing wars, inquisitions, crusades, jihads, prejudicial attitudes, terrorism, and intolerance (see recent work by C. Hitchens). The question, unfortunately, is fundamentally unanswerable without some means of measuring the impact of such behaviors, both good and bad. How, for example, is the value of religiously inspired works of art to be balanced against the human costs of wars and crusades? How can we quantify the many ways our spirits seem lifted by such achievements against the suffering caused by the violence? Absent some accounting method to help us accomplish this analysis, we simply cannot provide these answers, and I believe the debate to be pointless.

Unanswerable though such a question may be, however, it does raise a related one. Although we may not agree on whether, in balance, religious belief has been a positive or negative force in human history, we can probably all agree that religiously inspired strife has been an important part of human history. Why is this so? Why is religion often associated with the dark side of human behavior even while it can be an important source of inspiration?

4. How Epistemology and Behavior Are Intertwined

The answer to this puzzling question may lie in what religious claims are thought to represent. While how willing we are to use a belief as a warrant for our actions is probably related to how certain we are that it is true, the notion of absolute truth, often associated with religious doctrines, may lie at the bottom of this question. As we noted, the recognition of absolute truths in areas of inquiry lacking means of confirmation is an inevitable and fundamental source of human conflict, and it is precisely here that religion sows the seeds of human strife. Each of the three great monotheistic religious faiths, for example, holds as core tenets claims that are irreconcilable with the others.

As noted earlier, certitude over claims about the world is impossible without some means of checking their truth content, which then provides us an avenue for resolving differences of views. But in the case of religious doctrine, the founding "truths" are drawn from personal revelation or certainty about the veracity of sacred texts. Which claims are historically true? How could we decide? As a group we may individually disagree that removing heat from water eventually converts it from liquid to solid, but such an empirical question can be resolved experimentally, by turning to controlled observation, while fundamental religious disagreements seldom can be so resolved.

As a result, two difficulties are intertwined. The first is that many systems of religious belief include truth claims that conflict fundamentally and irreconcilably with those of other rival religions, and absent some form of objective verification, any reconciliation of these differences is impossible without one side or the other abandoning basic tenets. The second difficulty arises from our own (already discussed) unwillingness to abandon beliefs once we form them, a propensity complicated if that belief system promises its adherents certain rewards (such as immortality) or is perceived to be a source of personal strength that helps us to cope with personal hardship. In these cases, converting from one religious faith to another, even in the face of stronger, more credible evidence on behalf of a rival belief system, is a pill too bitter for many of us to swallow. In other words, such kinds of belief systems consist of fundamentally irreconcilable truth claims inherently immune to objective examination because at their core they are untestable, and yet they have undeniable appeal to their adherents because of advantages and enhancements believing in them is thought to deliver. Not only do we tend to cling to our fixed beliefs in general, we have special reason to do so in these cases.

Stephen Jay Gould, of course, famously resolved this challenge by advancing the proposition that science and religion represent "nonoverlapping magisteria" (NOMA). Science was to limit itself to empirical questions like what and where, while religion contended with questions of why and should, and as a result the two dealt with different kinds of inquiries. But others have questioned this partitioning because many religions draw their supposed moral authority directly from their empirical claims about revelations and interventions in a way that blurs the distinction between the two alleged magisteria.

Whatever one thinks of the NOMA proposition, because of the untestability of their core beliefs, religious adherents are frequently left unable to ascertain whether their deepest religious convictions are actually correct but are unlikely to abandon them even if they thought that they were, and yet they are held deeply and used as a warrant for actions. Unfortunately, others, holding just as passionately to religious views that are irreconcilably different, will act differently, opening the door to conflict. One need look no further than the contradictions nested within radical versions of Judaism, Islam, and Christianity for evidence.

The more general issue I am raising here has to do with what philosophers call the "ethics of belief," which arises because what one believes to be true about the world is related to how one acts. Whether individuals "fix" beliefs by leaps of faith (or by any other method) is a purely personal matter until such beliefs are used to guide their actions toward others; acting on false beliefs, according to this view, raises the probability of antisocial actions. If we believe (wrongly) that the worth of human beings is related to the color of their skin, for example, our actions are more likely to discriminate between individuals of different skin color.

For these reasons, then, the issue of how we come to believe what we do is not disconnected from how we treat others, especially if our "belief engines" are generating false convictions that lead us, in turn, to mistreat them, which is an ethical issue. To whatever extent our beliefs determine our treatment of others, and if we have some moral obligation to treat them as well as we can, then we have a resulting moral obligation to follow those belief-fixing methods that are most likely to generate true beliefs.

5. Further Hidden Costs of Religious Belief

As noted earlier, we humans excel at recognizing patterns amid sparse observations and weaving causal narratives around them, but unfortunately the religious among us then often stumble by identifying this cause as having agency rather than being naturalistic or mechanistic in nature, and we complicate our error by attributing human qualities to the agency. Evolutionary biologists might view such a tendency as genetically based, arising out of selective pressures operating in our remote past because they conferred some survival advantage among those members of our species who developed them at the time. Religious belief represents the full flowering of such a hard-wiring in our brains when we attribute benevolent purpose to what are objectively unrelated events and thus nurture what are in fact untrue beliefs about the world.

Holding such beliefs absent or contrary to evidence is not necessarily in every instance counterproductive for us, however, especially if they are either outcome-neutral (do not form a basis for our actions) or may just by accident be true. Nonetheless, in the long run, they are likely to yield suboptimal decisions (perhaps affecting our treatment of others) compared to beliefs grounded in evidence. For example, human rights initiatives promoting respect and equal status to all responsible members of our society (such as women and homosexuals) may be thwarted when their social status is understood to be defined solely by sacred texts that devalue such persons. Tradition-bound conceptions of the role of women in society are especially widespread in much of Islamic south Asia, for example, where culture and religious doctrine are mutually supporting, and such conceptions materially impede the transformation of the status of these groups along more Western outlines of equality. Given the uncontested a priori esteem in which such texts are often held, how can the truth of such views (and, hence, their suitability as a basis for action) be assessed except by resorting to empirical critique, which is contrary to the notion of a sacred text.

In addition, exactly *what* we believe on account of our religious views may serve us poorly in other ways as we navigate our way in the new "information age." How do we understand the meaning of new scientific discoveries around us? The stunning recent advances in molecular biology make the most sense in the context of macroevolutionary theory. Surely, evidence that we are descended from ancestors shared in common with chimpanzees sits very awkwardly with many who embrace prior and deeply held religious views that humans occupy a unique and special place on the earth. As a result of this conflict, no doubt some very bright minds are turned away from careers in biology or medical science. Might some of them hold the potential to develop important medical advances or even cures for dread diseases?

Surveys tell us that our willingness to embrace controversial scientific theories is related to the strength of religious belief. For example, various reports have suggested that creationist beliefs are more likely to be held by those with greater belief in God, or greater religious observance (in a study of the attitudes of teachers in Europe and North Africa). Teaching our young to rely on leaps of faith to fix beliefs may well undermine our wider commitment to rational, evidenced-based decision making, which is essential in many other areas of endeavor important in our lives (not only in science but also in the judicial system, for example).

All this is to point out that not only what we believe but also how our beliefs are acquired is not a trivial question and that some ways are preferable to others if we want our society to respect rational (evidence-based) inquiry that we value in nonreligious enterprises. Fostering such respect is difficult in a social climate that permits epistemological schizophrenia.

All in all, then, these considerations suggest that we can do better than look to religious faith for moral instruction and inculcation. Defenders of faith-based moral values like to point out that even if some of the core tenets of a religion turn out to be factually wrong, the moral principles associated with the religion remain valuable and continue to inspire many to virtue. If so, however, problems would remain "around the edge," where more extreme views based directly on scriptural interpretation have taken hold and are used to justify extreme behavior such as subservience of women or racial extremism. It is these costs, I argue, that could be avoided under other, more empirical belief-fixing models. As such, they, rather than a religious approach to incentivizing truthfulness, or morality in general, should win our assent hands down.

Some observers argue that religion provides answers to deep problems of human existence, such as meaning and purpose, that cannot be obtained by reliance only on a rational/scientific/materialist worldview like the one I am advocating. If this critique means to imply that only religion can supply meaning and purpose, it is contrary to the evidence, because millions of nonreligious Americans, not to mention many more in other parts of the world, go about their lives with meaning and purpose every day, obviously having derived it elsewhere. Other critics claim that, without God, morality would degenerate into fashion and relativism, with nothing forbidden. A set of moral principles, in other words, would be untethered and, with no limits, be free to drift into some caricature of itself. This view, too, is mistaken.

To the contrary, the checks and balances needed to prevent such a slide into relativism as well as provide us with a reason to help others, which then anchor our lives with transcendent purpose, originate from empathy. Feeling the pain of others prompts us to want to help them, and nurturing without religion the skills of empathetic identification, especially among our young, would go far in softening the rough edges of modern egoistic, market-fostered ethics. In other words, while being empathetic would have little influence on what kind of ethical system we each prefer to follow, it would help assure that we maintain focus on the end product of lessening the pain or enhancing the well-being of others. While I grant that some individuals may indeed be motivated to "be moral" by religious beliefs, I think that, imbued with empathetic insight, we are more likely to grasp the many ways our actions have potential to hurt others and, hence, to modulate them, and this special ability, more than any other, anchors moral principles in general. Rather than promoting religion, I think we would do better by nurturing empathy, because doing so is not associated with any of the unintended negative consequences we see with the embrace of traditional religious belief.

Finally, as the focus of this piece has been on the connection between truthfulness and trust, and its intent is to argue that corrupting one undermines the other, we have viewed adherence to religious doctrine rather unfavorably as a panacea to creeping untruthfulness. This discussion then led us into a more general critique of religion as a positive force in the modern world. For many of us religious skeptics, conservatives, and not a few moderates alike, the rise of Islamic fundamentalism/extremism that we are now witnessing in parts of the world is particularly worrying. Unfortunately, the prevalence of Christian fundamentalism in our own culture frequently passes with barely a comment in the mainstream media, and political candidates often seem to be in a contest to see who can wear their religion most proudly in public.

What is widely missed in this spectacle, of course, is the recognition of a double standard: even moderate Christians adhere to religious views that suffer from the same kind of defect that characterizes the fundamentalism they so fear. As I pointed out elsewhere, by committing to one particular version of religious truth they are denying the truth of other views (when they embrace mutually exclusive claims that cannot all be true), a particularly egregious oversight when objective, warranted certainty in any interpretation is impossible. Furthermore, with such a move they are laying the groundwork for a hierarchy that places themselves, by virtue of the "truth" of their own beliefs, above others who hold differing views. From here, acting on the basis of this hierarchy (by denigrating, demonizing, or discriminating against those others) is only a small additional step.

Allowing ourselves to believe that we (and not others) are in possession of such a thing as Absolute Truth without a means to confirm is a recipe for division and conflict between in-groups and out-groups. Religious conservatives claim that Darwin's theory of evolution was a "dangerous idea," but I think they are, well, dead wrong. The really dangerous idea, perhaps the most dangerous idea in the history of human thought, is in the existence of an Absolute Truth when it leads to certainty where we cannot be sure. Certainty closes minds and invites conflict, whereas doubt nurtures curiosity and opportunity.

7 Concluding Thoughts

Ideas have consequences if they change the way enough people look at the world, and people then change their own behavior as a result. Our confidence that this is so drives so many of our actions. We debate with others, instruct our children, and go to sometimes great lengths to preserve our thoughts in writing for posterity, all on the conviction that what we say matters. Whether any particular idea lives up to its potential to change the course of things depends, of course, on many imponderables, not the least of which is how the idea is received among the population in the first place. That, in turn, reflects at least in part the historical contingency of the time.

The importance of being truthful is a small and modest idea at best. Trite in the extreme, we hear it from our parents, teachers, and clergy persons, and it is not difficult to do. And yet, it increasingly seems to be a neglected virtue, at least in our political discourse. Perhaps the problem with truthfulness, after all, is little more than the obscured nature of the harm violating it does. If so, if perhaps a bit of sunshine is all that is needed to broaden our appreciation of its harms, then my objective here has been to place it back on the table for general consideration as the core and bedrock virtue communicating animals all share. Failing to do so, I believe, imperils much of what we value in our modern society.

References

Frankfurt, Harry G. 2006. *On Truth*. New York: Alfred A. Knopf.

Habermas, Jurgen. 1990. *Moral Consciousness and Communicative Action*. Translated by C. Lenhardt and S. Nicholson. Cambridge, MA: MIT Press.

Jacoby, Susan. 2004. *Freethinkers: A History of American Secularism*. New York: Metropolitan Books.

Kurtz, Paul. 2009. "The future of secular humanism in America." *Free Inquiry* 29 (5): 4–8.

MacIntyre, Alasdair. 1984. *After Virtue*. Notre Dame, IN: Notre Dame Press.

———. 1988. *Whose Justice? Whose Rationality?* Notre Dame, IN: Notre Dame Press.

Mooney, Chris. 2005. *The Republican War on Science*. New York: Basic Books.

Nozick, Robert. 1993. *The Nature of Rationality*. Princeton, NJ: Princeton University Press.

Pigliucci, Massimo. 2009. "The moral duty of a skeptic." *Skeptical Inquirer* 33 (6): 18–19.

Singer, Peter. 2000. *Writings on an Ethical Life*. New York: Harper Collins.

Zuckerman, Phil. 2006. "Is faith good for us?" *Free Inquiry* 26 (5): 35–38.

"Crossing the divide." *Science* 319 (22 February 2008): 1034–36.

About the Author

Jay R. Harman is professor emeritus in the Department of Geography at Michigan State University, where his early research and teaching specialties included climatology and plant geography of North America. His award-winning skill in the classroom and numerous publications in his specialties resulted in disciplinary recognition, but these successes left him craving more classroom flexibility to discuss questions of value and meaning that students increasingly seemed to be asking. Eventually, he abandoned his traditional specialties for an evolving interest in ethical philosophy by teaching and writing in the field of environmental ethics. This focus, in turn, led him toward more general inquiry into applied ethics and ultimately into the subject of this book. It represents, he says, years of reflection on what he sees as the corrosive influence of untruthfulness in popular political discourse in America today, and it is a logical end point to the arc of his personal journey as an academician. Currently, Jay lives on an acreage outside of Lansing, MI, with his wife, daughters, and their dog Sable, where they keep bees and chickens, garden, and oversee their renewable energy systems.

About the Book

This book is an inquiry into the harms being done by untruthfulness in American popular political discourse today and how we might arrest them. Taking the form of claims and counterclaims, this untruthfulness is both accidental and intentional and is transmitted in a myriad of media outlets as well as (and especially) by politicians themselves. In turn, we, as consumers of these products, face the daunting task of separating truth from spin, hyperbole, half-truths, and outright prevarication. With the proliferation of various fact-checking websites on the Internet, one might think that corroborating the accuracy of various claims is easier than ever. Unfortunately, many of us seem just as ready to accept the line from partisan websites and agenda-driven think tanks as we are to ferret out alternative interpretations, leaving us with views that are often reinforced rather than tested and unable to distinguish fact from fiction. As a result, untruths and exaggeration, once planted in the public narrative, acquire lives of their own in subsequent discourse. There is no wonder that polls consistently show that Americans are confused about basic issues or policies and even scientific facts themselves.

All of this is more than an annoyance if it cripples our performance as voters. How can we be expected to make informed choices at the polls if we are befuddled by what we read or hear? And if we are befuddled, how can we be expected to identify those candidates most likely to lead our democracy forward in the twenty-first century?

Collateral Damage considers the many forms untruthfulness assumes in public discourse, why it seems to be so common and widespread, and offers some suggestions on how we might address it. While the author jokes that this book may appear to be little more than the machinations of a third-rate mind, it is heartfelt and on-target, nonetheless.

Acknowledgments

Many people have contributed, directly or indirectly, to the effort and inspiration needed for me to publish this book, and this account doubtlessly overlooks some of them. I first would like to acknowledge the folks at AuthorHouse for their guidance and assistance at several stages in the publication process. Beforehand, however, the manuscript had to be written and revised, a task that would have been difficult without the support of the Department of Geography, Michigan State University. They helped it happen by providing me office space and computer support as a newly retired faculty member. Among my many colleagues there, noted author and Departmental colleague Harm de Blij offered early encouragement and useful suggestions, not to mention serving as an important role model in the publishing arena. I am indebted to him for the numerous conversations we had over the last few years about the whole matter. My jogging partner, Dr. Ronald Marshall, and I shared many, sometimes heated, conversations about social policy as we loped around the MSU campus, and I learned much from his economics perspective. Of the few individuals with whom I actually shared copies of early drafts of this book, Aron Thomas, a former student, was particularly generous with his time and effort in making suggestions or raising questions. Doug Pearson, another former student, succeeded at publishing his own book and helped show me how easy it is to do such things these days. Kerry Shadbolt perceptively captured the desired nuance in her artwork for the book's cover. Along the way, and going back to the early years, I was inspired by some very good teachers, particular Robert J. "Sam" Phillips. As a high school senior, I learned to appreciate the virtue of "thinking for oneself" that he so often emphasized. Without doubt, he impacted me more than any other teacher ever did, and his legacy lives on in these pages. Finally, my wife Theresa and children Sara and Rachel were, and remain, a reason for me to get up in the morning and pursue my scholarly agenda in the first place, and my indebtedness to them is not trivial.

www.ingramcontent.com/pod-product-compliance
Lightning Source LLC
Chambersburg PA
CBHW050400290526
45786CB00003B/1062